THE COSTUME MAKING GUIDE

Creating Armor & Props for Cosplay

Svetlana Quindt
aka **Kamui Cosplay**

IMPACT
CINCINNATI, OHIO
www.impact-books.com

What You Need

Materials
- Balsa wood
- Craft foam
- EVA foam
- PVC pipes
- Worbla, black and brown

Paints and Glues
- Acrylic paint
- Automotive spray primer
- Brush cleaner or turpentine substitute
- Contact cement
- Lacquer
- Nail polish
- Plasti Dip
- Rub'n Buff
- Spray paint
- Varnish
- White glue

Tools
- Assorted brushes
- Craft knife or box cutter
- Dremel
- Dust mask and safety glasses
- Heat gun
- Hot glue gun and sticks
- Old socks / lint-free fabric
- Paper
- Pens / markers
- Pins
- Ruler
- Sandpaper
- Scissors
- Water-soluble pen or chalk

Miscellaneous
- D-rings, Velcro, furniture leather and buckles
- Duct tape
- Magnets
- Parting wax
- Plastic wrap
- Resin gemstones
- Spherical piece of plastic, metal or pottery
- Vacuum cleaner

Contents

How to Create a Bracer   24
Basic techniques from pattern making and
shaping Worbla to priming, painting with
acrylics, sealing and creating attachments

How to Create a Breastplate   48
Working with EVA foam, sealing with
Plasti Dip and applying spray paint

How to Create a Pauldron   64
Shaping Worbla, applying and sanding spray filler
and automotive spray paint

How to Create an Axe   76
Creating an EVA foam axe from a
blueprint to the final prop

How to Create a Sword   90
Combining balsa wood and Worbla
for prop creation

A Complete Costume
From Start to Finish   100
The entire construction process of a cosplay
from the first thought to the final photo

What's Next   108
What to do once you've made your epic costume

Costume Inspiration Gallery   112
More inspiring costumes by talented artists

About This Book

Many people love watching movies. Some like to play video games. Others spend their free time reading comic books. A few also write their own stories, draw their own comic books or film their own videos. And some people spend their time creating costumes and turning into superheroes over the weekend!

Over the last few years, cosplay has become a way of life for a whole generation spread all over the world. Youngsters and seniors alike hide in their workshops for weeks and months only to emerge in impressive and elaborate outfits. There are even some kids who craft mighty armor sets for their parents. Cosplay is a hobby that connects people no matter their age, gender or skin color.

The fact that you're holding this book in your hands right now makes me excited that you want to join our crafty and creative community. If you are already familiar with cosplay, then you know how much fun dressing up and playing pretend can be. If you are not, then let me welcome you with open arms. I'll see you in costume by the end of the book.

The guides in this book won't directly transform you into a giant robot, but I will show you the techniques you need to turn yourself into one. I'm not a seamstress though, so this book will focus on cool armor pieces and elaborate props. You won't learn how to master a sewing machine, but I will guide you through the planning of a costume and will teach you all kinds of different crafting techniques. I will show you how to turn plain foam into a realistic axe and how to create an amazing breastplate from scratch.

Bringing your dreams to life with your own two hands is an amazing experience I want to share with you. With cosplay you can become anyone or anything you want!

Photo by Darshelle Stevens: darshellestevens.com

Introducing the Author

Hi there! I'm Svetlana, but most people know me under my artist name: Kamui. Even though I'm about to teach you how to create your own costumes, I'm still just a girl from Germany who spends all of her free time building stuff and dressing up. I discovered this hobby back in 2003 when I read about cosplay in a journal about anime and manga. Creating outfits of my favorite characters was an idea I instantly fell in love with, and a few weeks later I had already put together my very first self-made costume from the anime *Dragon Ball Z*. I had such a great time with my friends at my very first convention (a type of fan gathering) and also learned what cosplay really is about—having fun and connecting with like-minded people.

From that point on there was no turning back. My costumes became more and more elaborate, and over time I began sharing my self-taught techniques on the Internet to help and to inspire the community that I've learned so much from. I strongly believe that sharing what we know with others makes the world more fun. Everybody had a helping hand at some point in their life, and passing this on to others around you is the best way to return the favor. To do this in a meaningful way I am writing my own handy crafting books that have already found their way into countless households around the globe.

Besides writing guides and working on new costumes, conventions also invite me to travel all over the United States, Europe and Asia to run panels and workshops. I love discovering new places and meeting inspiring people, so hopefully we will meet one day, wherever and whenever this may be!

To see more of my work, visit www.kamuicosplay.com.

What Is Cosplay?

While cosplay has really exploded in the last few years, it's not at all a new phenomenon. It was the year 1939 when Myrtle R. Jones first created a gown for herself and a rugged looking star pilot costume for her friend Forrest J. Ackerman. With their re-creations of the costumes from the classic film *Things to Come*, both of them were stars among the casually dressed gathering of writers, artists and fans at their local convention. They inspired the science fiction community to change the serious image they had up to this point. One year later the first Worldcon masquerade was held, though it was still more of a costume ball with prizes at the end.

In the following decades the popularity of costume fandom in North America exploded, and *Star Trek* and *Star Wars* especially helped to boost the idea of dressing up as your favorite character. In 1983 Nobuyuki Takahashi from the Japanese media outlet Studio Hard attended Worldcon in Los Angeles and was instantly impressed by all the colorful and elaborate costumes spread all over the convention hall. Using the term *cosplay*—based on *costume* and *play*—he reported about this phenomenon in the Japanese journal *My Anime,* which set the initial spark for readers in Japan to dress up as well. Since then *cosplay* has become the term for one of the most passionate ways to express your fandom.

Cosplay Contests

Since the first masquerade was held in 1940, elaborate costume contests have become a big highlight at many international conventions and inspire participants to create more and more impressive projects. Even if you are not into competing, there is no shortage of people just loving the experience of creating a costume with their own two hands.

While cosplay and costuming steadily grew in North America and Asia, the TV premiere of Japanese anime like *Sailor Moon* in the 1990s gave the international community another huge boost. Inspired girls all over the world started to dress up in Japanese school uniforms. After this show finally aired in Europe, countless new fans discovered the fascination for dressing up as their favorite characters.

In 2003, the first prestigious World Cosplay Summit (WCS) was held in Nagoya, Japan. This worldwide contest run by the Japanese channel TV Aichi began their festivities with cosplayers from four countries only, though more and more nationalities joined over the years. Today the WCS has become a weeklong event with twenty-eight participating nations spread all over the globe. Following its success, the event became an inspiration for further international contests like the European Cosplay Gathering or the C2E2 Crown Championships of Cosplay in North America.

With the Internet making cosplay accessible to everybody, the culture received another huge boost, especially over the last ten years. Downloadable fan translations of anime and community platforms like cosplay.com and deviantart.com helped the idea of dressing up grow and spread all over the globe. All kinds of online shops for crafting materials, wigs and even full costumes made the hobby more accessible and inspired countless new people to dress up for the very first time. Some cosplayers began creating tutorials and writing blogs, which made it so

Cosplayers: Lupin Cosplay & Lillyn Cosplay | Photo by: CoolADN

much easier to get into this amazing hobby. The world has become a place full of inspiration where talented artists can share their ideas with other people thousands of miles away.

No one has to hide their geeky side—if you still enjoy playing Pokémon at the age of fifty, or if you watch *Game of Thrones* for an entire weekend, or even if you're jumping around in a tight, rainbow-colored superhero bodysuit in public—it's totally okay. Share your passion with others! We're all dungeon masters, live action role players, video gamers, readers and movie lovers. Be proud of who you are, take a selfie and love and support other members of the community the same way. It's a crazy and beautiful world out there!

Photo by FiveRings Photography

Why Cosplay?

For me personally, cosplay is the strongest and purest way to express your love for a fandom. Creating a costume from scratch by spending days and nights with your sewing machine or heat gun and using most of your hard-earned money to bring this dream to life takes passion and pure dedication. Before cosplay you just consumed the art and worlds of other artists by reading comics, watching movies or playing video games, but now you're becoming the artist yourself!

It's important to understand that a costume will not be done overnight. Well, at least most of them won't be. Cosplayers often spend months and all of their pocket money on elaborate armor sets, fully animated light suits or hand-sculpted silicone rubber monsters. In Hollywood, huge costume design teams are responsible for dressing up the actors for movies, while a cosplayer is able to re-create the same project in a much smaller room with fewer professional tools and all by himself. No matter how complicated, weird and detailed a character concept is, there will always be a highly motivated cosplayer somewhere who takes on the challenge and makes it possible.

There are many different reasons why we choose to dress up as a certain character. It may be the interesting personality or just the look that you adore. Some people go as far as to adopt the character's behaviors, speech and body language. They become their heroes and try to walk in their shoes at least for a few days. Didn't we all wonder at some point what it would feel like to save the world as Spider-Man or Wonder Woman?

There are other cosplayers who simply enjoy being creative. They want the challenge and pick projects out of their skill set and comfort zone. Creating a piece of art, little by little, with their own hands, and seeing it grow and develop is their way of expressing themselves.

Having Fun Together

In the early days of the hobby, crafting instructions and useful tutorials were very hard to come by. Materials and tools first had to be discovered and new skills had to be learned. Every new project raised further questions and required a different skill. Sewing a gown, wig styling, special-effect makeup, sculpting, molding, casting and even working with electronics or real steel—over the years cosplayers became masters of countless crafting techniques. Today we enjoy sharing our knowledge with the rest of the community over social media and various other platforms.

Many of us were geeks or outsiders at school and had trouble finding real friends. Cosplay—maybe the most nerdy hobby

(Above) Kamui Cosplay with Mario and Alice Roy from Arms, Armor and Awesome. (Top right, from left to right) Lightning Cosplay, Shellshocked Cosplay, Ardsami Cosplay, NoFace Cosplay, Lime Cosplay and Kamui Cosplay. (Bottom right) Kamui Cosplay and Selina Bäumler.

of them all—changed this drastically. Conventions are not only an amazing place to present costumes but also an amazing opportunity to meet like-minded people who share your passion and love. It's the only place on earth where someone recognizes your costume even if your character appeared in only a single panel of a comic.

Cosplaying in groups has become highly popular and is an opportunity to find lifelong friends. Having crafting sessions at home or over the Internet, sharing materials and suffering together through sleepless nights until you can finally present your finished costumes is highly addicting. Some members of the community are so busy with their plans that they become masters of time management. With dozens of projects planned with different people and for different events, the question "So what's your next costume?" might take a while to answer.

Social media is undeniably one of the biggest influences on the cosplay community today. The ability to share your own work and follow other artists basically opened a brand new world and connected the community. While you are surrounded with friends during the day, it can still get pretty lonely when you craft in your basement. The Internet and especially social media are there to help you out. These days we're able to share our costume crafting photos on Facebook, post silly selfies with our pets in costumes on Instagram and upload detailed tutorial videos on YouTube. It doesn't matter anymore what part of the world you are from, what race or sex you are or what cultural environment you've grown up in—our love for cosplay connects us!

Choosing a Costume

A cosplayer's wish list is often so long that it easily fills the schedule for the next couple of years. As a newcomer though, you might ask, "What should I cosplay?" Let me lend you a helping hand.

When it comes to this question, the best answer is probably to do what you love. If you're a fan of a TV show or a comic book, why not dress up as your favorite hero? As a video game fan you surely already know a nice armor set or weapon that you always wanted to have for your own, right? The characters described in books can be a great choice, too. If you have a specific image of how Daenerys Targaryen from *A Song of Ice and Fire* should have looked, then that's a good start. Some people also create original characters, animals or even general themes like seasons, foods or colors.

Cosplay is fun, so just do whatever you want to do. It's also all about you, so there is no need to look like the spitting image of a character. We're just human. No one is Batman, has the muscles of Hulk or is born with the crazy, unrealistic wasp waist that so many heroines have. Tony Stark can be a girl, and Wonder Woman can also be African-American or Asian. Being an artist means being free to express yourself and not be bound by skin color, sex or body shape. Dress up as whoever you want to be and enjoy all the different character interpretations you'll find on the convention floor. You might even discover some inspiration for one of your next projects.

Finding Good Reference Material

Once you have decided on a costume, it's time to try to get a good look at it—from head to toe. What materials and fabrics do you need? Do you have to wear a wig or are you considering just getting the right hairstyle yourself? The best way to find this out is by collecting good reference pictures of your character. It's pretty tough to build Wonder Woman's breastplate if you have no idea how it looks from the back.

Hitting up the Internet is usually the first stop to find all kinds of nice reference materials. You'll be surprised how much you can get if you just know where to look.

First off, Google is your best friend. The image search function will provide you with countless pictures and websites that will help you narrow down the right materials, colors and hairstyles. It's also worth checking out other places. Pinterest might have useful movie replica photos or otherwise unreleased material. Artists on deviantart.com show off their own interpretations and might provide you with an entirely fresh view of your character of choice. Last but not least, YouTube is an amazing platform to discover three-dimensional turntables or other video references.

Aside from the Internet, colorful artbooks might give you completely new ideas as well. They are full of stunning illustrations and inspiring concept artwork. Same goes for action figurines, which will not only give you a full, clear view all around your character but also clear three-dimensional shapes, textures and size dimensions of various costume pieces.

It's quite helpful to see every angle of your costume before you actually start a project. The more research material you have, the easier your work will be in the end.

Searching for Inspiration

You'll notice pretty quickly that the cosplay community is an amazing place to look for support. If you're having trouble with sewing, are not able to find the right material for your costume or are stuck with a problem in general, you'll always find a helping hand. Keep your eyes open and ask around.

Just type cosplay tutorial into the Google search bar, and you'll end up with countless step-by-step instructions for props and full costumes, detailed photo stories of how to style your wig, and guides on different topics like costume transportation, installing lights or even how to prepare a cosplay skit. There is no need to reinvent the wheel. Just the fact that you're holding this book in your hands right now shows how easy it is to find help for working creatively. Besides all this, you'll find countless other publications about sewing, embroidery, prop making, special effects, makeup and much more.

We live in a world where you can basically learn everything from your home just by doing your homework and spending your time with proper research. Everything is right there in front of you. You just need to pick your favorite technique and go nuts.

Even if you still end up getting stuck, just ask around the community and somebody will eventually come to your rescue. We all started small, after all!

What You Need to Get Started

Before we can start working on our first projects, we'll need some tools and materials. Crafting is an essential part of cosplay, and there are a thousand ways to achieve what you want to create. Nevertheless, there are a few basic things that every cosplayer should have available. For this reason I've prepared a short shopping list for you over the following pages. Don't worry though, I stayed pretty cost conscious. This addictive hobby will start to torture your purse soon enough, so for now we'll keep it easy.

There is one more thing I should mention. Since I currently live in Germany and buy most of my materials at local shops, there may be a few products that will look or sound different than the materials you get in your country. During my travels in the last couple of years, I visited a lot of different shops and hardware stores to make sure everything I cover in this book is readily available pretty much everywhere. Sometimes products carry different names, but the way they work stays the same, so there is nothing to worry about. You just have to find them.

Useful Tools and Materials

Worbla and Worbla's Black Art

This thermoplastic material comes in brown or black sheets of different sizes. It can be cut with regular scissors and heated up with an ordinary heat gun. Once the material reaches around 176° F (80° C), it becomes flexible like fabric and activates a glue that makes it stick to itself. Simply press it together to get a strong and lasting connection. Shape it while it's still hot, and once it has cooled down Worbla will stay in this new shape. Additionally, you can heat it up as many times as you want, which makes the material very forgiving. Your result is super durable and will last an eternity. It still has a few disadvantages though. Brown Worbla has a rough, sand-like texture, so you need to apply a primer before you're able to paint your work. The new black alternative tries to remedy this, though the glue within isn't as strong in comparison. Both materials are quite popular and you can find countless crafting tutorials online.

Craft Foam and EVA Foam

Many of us still remember craft foam from our childhood. It's not only very easy to find but is a super affordable material. Despite being really basic, it's quite handy for a lot of applications. If your budget is limited, you can even create entire costumes out of it. Try to find large sheets or even rolls to minimize leftovers. Craft foam's big brother, EVA foam, is a bit harder to get. There are literally countless chemical variations of this material—some are soft, some are hard, some are heavy and some are lightweight. It's up to you to find which version you like the most, but the most commonly used foams for cosplay are black floor mats and EVA foam called L200. Shops like Amazon and eBay are usually the right place to find both craft and EVA foam, though it's also worth checking out craft and hardware stores. For your costumes I recommend getting a couple different foams to choose from.

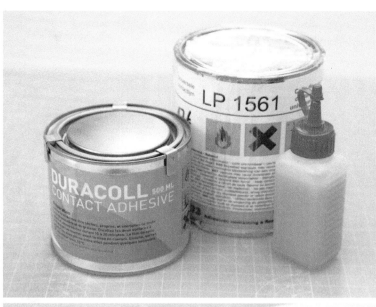

Contact Cement

Working with wood, foam and plastic sheets usually requires a special type of glue with an extra strong connection. Contact cement is the solution. It's a viscous, air-drying glue that needs to be applied in a thin layer to both of the pieces that you want to stick together. Let it dry for a couple of minutes until the surface is slightly sticky. Afterwards press these two parts together and their connection will hold for an eternity. It's a must-have for every foam project since the bond is so strong that you will not be able to tear it apart without damaging the foam itself. Usually shops that offer EVA foam also sell this glue. As an alternative, search for a product called Barge cement.

Balsa Wood

While mainly used for architecture miniatures, balsa wood is also great for cosplay. It's soft and lightweight like Styrofoam and can be bought in handy planks of different lengths and thicknesses—just perfect for all kinds of blades. While regular wood is hard to shape without the right tools, balsa is soft enough that you can cut it with a hobby knife or simply sand it with sandpaper. The material is not very durable, though, and breaks easily under a bit of pressure. You'll find a simple solution for this in the sword tutorial later in the book. Balsa planks are mostly available in online shops and usually on eBay; however, it's possible that your local craft store offers them as well.

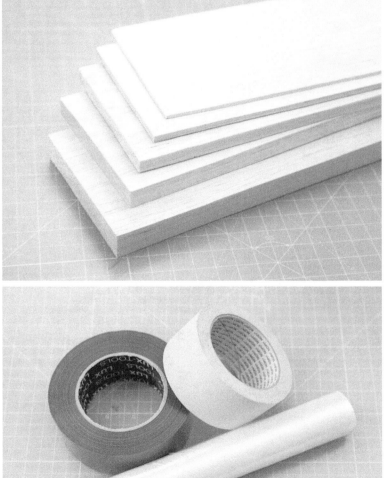

Plastic Wrap and Tape

You always need a pattern before you can start building any kind of armor. The easiest technique is basically to wrap yourself in plastic wrap and duct tape and draw on the shape you want. This also works perfectly for patterns on shirts, coats and all kinds of fabric projects. Using this technique you can plan and design even elaborate dresses with a perfect fit. Since we will need this quite regularly, stock up on wrap and tape from your nearest supermarket. Duct tape is not a must since most tapes work just fine for this, as long as you're still able to cut yourself free afterward.

Paints and Brushes

It might take a while until you find a brand of paint that you really like. I usually work with high pigment acrylics from Amsterdam as well as from Reeves, since these colors have a very high viscosity and need only one or two coats to get a shiny covering of paint. For special metal effects, Rub'n Buff is great as well. High-quality acrylics might be a bit more expensive, but usually the money you spend for the colors shortens the amount of time you need to spend applying them. A good alternative is spray cans, though you'll need a well-ventilated area to work with them. While chrome and shiny reflective gold will be hard to achieve with regular acrylics, spray paint will give you a perfect result in no time. As for the brushes, try to get some soft, high-quality brushes in all sizes but don't spend too much on them as you will wear them out fairly quickly.

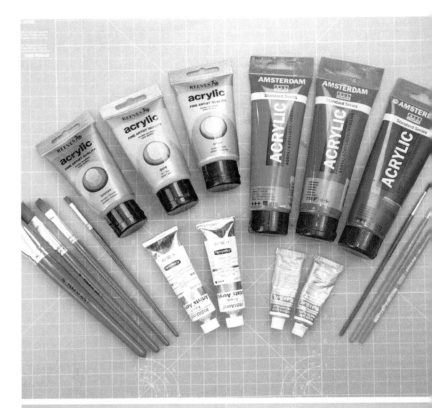

White Glue and Plasti Dip

Most of the time you will need to prime your Worbla or EVA foam before you can give it a nice coat of paint. This gives your armor piece or prop a smooth and shiny surface and your colors something to hold onto. What primer to use depends on your material of choice. If you're working with Worbla, you'll need something thick like the good old white glue (Elmer's glue). A few coats of this stuff will turn your rough sandy surface into a shiny and polished piece—just like real metal. If you are working with foam, then don't forget to buy some Plasti Dip. Made for the car industry, it's basically a brush-on or spray-on rubber coat. By applying a few thin coats you can turn your soft and delicate foam build into a flexible and durable armor piece. Additionally it's available in many different colors, which is really helpful for the upcoming paint job.

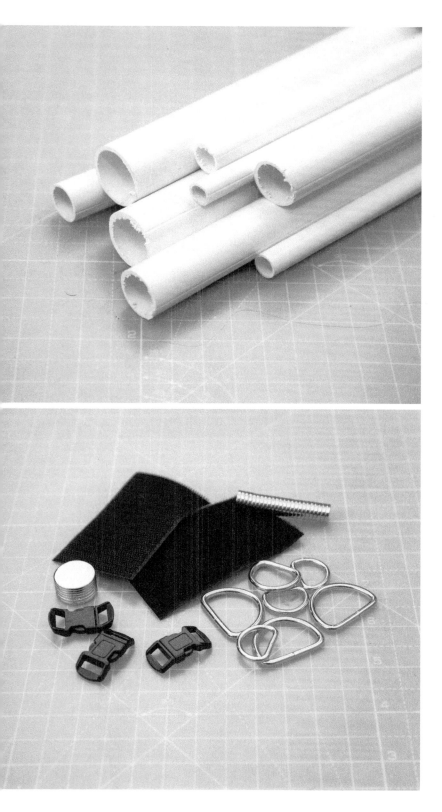

PVC Pipes

Swords, axes and wands usually have some type of handle. A great solution for this is to use a simple PVC pipe from your local hardware store. Ask the staff for a few pipes in different thicknesses and lengths. They are not only cheap but also lightweight and easy to saw in half. You are even able to bend them with the help of your trusty heat gun. PVC pipes are always handy to have. You never know when you need to build a sword for the impending zombie apocalypse, right? Depending on your project, diameters of 1/2" to 1 1/4" (1–3cm) are usually enough for most props.

D-Rings, Velcro and Buckles

Every cool armor piece needs a proper attachment. In this book I'll show you some easy solutions, that usually work with D-rings, Velcro tape, buckles and rare earth magnets. If you're lucky, you can find all of this stuff in your local craft store though they might be limited in size and variety. Online stores like eBay and Amazon not only have countless different products, they also often offer better prices. You don't really need everything shown here, but it's always helpful to have more options available. The day will surely come when a tiny lost D-ring will be your last chance to finish a costume just in time before the convention starts.

Scissors, Box Cutters and Knives

A strong pair of scissors is essential for most crafting projects. Try to find one that is not only fine cutting simple paper, but also gets through thick foam and plastic. Keep them sharp by using a sharpener or some sandpaper. I highly recommend getting an extra pair just to cut fabrics and wigs since thick materials like Worbla, plastic and cardboard will probably mess those up after a while. If you mostly want to work with thick EVA foam mats, it's best to invest in some trusty box cutters and craft knives instead. A long sharp blade will provide nice clean cuts and will be super helpful for countless projects. Just keep in mind that working with foam will quickly dull your blade. So have your sharpener ready and try to use it regularly.

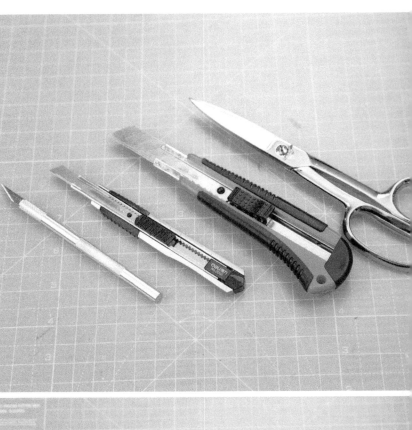

Heat Gun

You'll find heat guns in a wide range of strengths in almost every local hardware store. They work just like normal hair dryers except they're a lot hotter. The stronger versions usually cost a bit more, though it's worth it to invest in a quality product. Less power means shaping materials like Worbla and EVA foam will take longer and might drain your nerves. With a good heat gun in your workshop, you'll be able to heat and bend all kinds of thermoplastic materials fast and build your props and armor pieces in no time. As an advanced builder it's also not a bad idea to level up your dual-wielding ability and get a second heat gun. This will allow you to not only heat your material up much faster but also prepare you for every spontaneous crafting party with your best friend.

Markers, Pens and Rulers

For some crazy reason pens and rulers always disappear when you need them, so make sure to have at least a few lying around within reach. Get a variety of markers, pencils, ball pens and something waterproof as well. When working with a lot of different materials, you'll notice quickly that not everything draws on everything. Large metal rulers are not only great to set markings, but will especially help you to cut and shape EVA foam with ease. Simply put, just grab a bit of everything and you're set to start your first project. Over time you'll surely add more and more, but for now you'll most likely be fine with what you have at home.

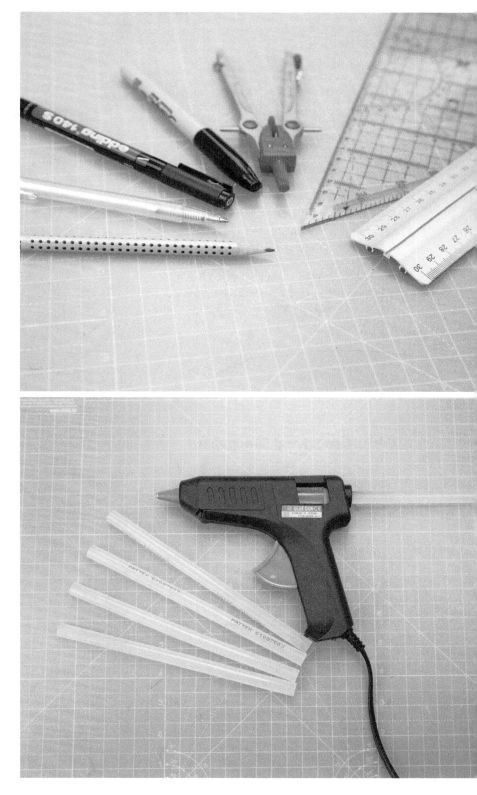

Hot Glue Gun

Hot glue is awesome. It's cheap, quick and can save you from countless tough spots. No doubt it will become your best friend pretty quickly! While a hot glue gun does not look like much, it can turn a boring dress into a glitter wonderland or help you fix almost every costume accident in no time. Always have some spare glue sticks ready and don't forget to turn it off after your crafting sessions. Be prepared to burn yourself every once in a while and note that it will probably not stick to everything in your workshop. In thirteen years of cosplay though, I haven't found a more useful and affordable tool.

Dremel

One of your favorite crafting tools will undoubtedly be the Dremel. With many different tips and sanding drums it's simply perfect for costume making. Using this versatile bad boy, you're able to sand, saw, drill, polish, sculpt and much more. You can add interesting and realistic textures, smooth out rough surfaces, hide visible seams or simply clean up messy cutting lines. Every tip gives you new ways to work creatively. To a beginner, a Dremel might seem like an advanced tool, but I promise you will never regret this purchase. Think about getting a shaft attachment as well. It's basically a handy extension that not only allows you to work more precisely, but is also much smaller and more lightweight than the original rotary tool.

Orbital Sander and Sandpaper

Sandpaper is really useful for tons of different applications. You can shape wood and foam, smooth out all kinds of materials and even sharpen your knives and scissors. You'll find sandpaper in all kinds of grits and variations, but I mainly use some with a grit between 80 and 240. A low number is perfect to get rid of a lot of material, while something like 240 is really fine and works perfectly for polishing. If you're keen on getting even more professional tools, an orbital sander would be a smart investment. It does not replace sanding by hand completely, but it will speed up your work considerably. Additionally, bigger projects with large sanding areas might not only drive you crazy from hand sanding, but might also harm your joints in the long run.

Safety First!

It's very important to be aware that while you're working on your projects you might have to handle fumes from spray cans and sticky glues and a lot of dust blown up by all the sanding. You will probably also cut and burn yourself every now and then. It's nothing unusual or terribly dangerous, and every good costume contains a little bit of blood, sweat and tears. Just try to concentrate and don't expose yourself to unnecessary risks if you don't have to. Before you actually start a project, get some standard safety equipment.

Respiratory protection should be number one on your list. A simple dust mask will protect your lungs when you're sanding, and opening a window has never hurt anyone either. There are special products that will protect you from toxic spray can fumes or certain types of glues, so try to look up what you need before you start working with something new.

Eye protection is also necessary for working with your Dremel or orbital sander as tiny pieces may come flying towards your eyes. Ear protection is important for loud machines, and gloves will save your fingers from being full of glue after a long crafty day. Just ask your local hardware store employee if you're ever unsure about what to get. They will surely love to help you out.

Materials

- Craft foam
- Worbla (brown)

Paints and Glues

- Acrylic paints
- Varnish
- White glue

Tools

- Assorted brushes
- Black marker
- Dremel
- Dust mask and safety glasses
- Heat gun
- Heat-resistant silicone mat (optional)
- Hot glue gun and sticks
- Pen and paper
- Scissors

Miscellaneous

- D-rings and a satin ribbon
- Duct tape
- Plastic wrap
- Resin gemstones
- Tissue Paper

How to Create a Bracer

Getting into cosplay without any experience or background knowledge isn't easy—especially if your dream costume is something elaborate, huge or really detailed. If you know the right tricks and techniques however, even the biggest, craziest projects will be child's play. So now it's finally time to start crafting. Grab your scissors, plug in your heat gun and get ready!

To give you an easy-to-follow introduction to all important techniques of cosplay armor making, I thought it would be a good idea to show you how to build something very simple that you'll need for almost every costume—a bracer. We'll start by creating the basic pattern, go over how to shape the material and finish it by adding details and giving it a nice paint job. Bracers are great for trying out new things, and they make a perfect first example. You can build this little armor piece super fast and won't lose too much material if you need a second try.

Drafting Basic Patterns

While armor patterns do not end up as a visible part of your final costume, creating them will be an amazing help in defining the shape and size of your final piece. They are basically the sketch of your finished artwork—you can't live without them. If you feel really impatient you can obviously just start playing around with material, but having a plan is never a bad idea. Luckily

there is an easy, quick and cheap way to get a perfect pattern for almost every armor piece you can imagine. All you need is some plastic wrap, duct tape, a marker and paper. Additionally a helping hand of a friend is really useful since cutting yourself free is sometimes more tricky than you might imagine.

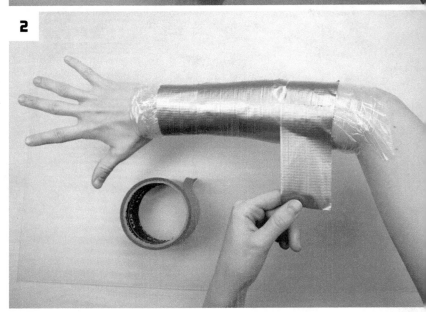

1 Wrap Your Arm in Plastic Wrap

Wrap the part of your body that you want to get armored. In this example it's your right forearm. Plastic wrap is perfect for this job, so just cover your arm with one or two tight layers. Make sure to add a few more inches (or several centimeters) over your wrist and elbow.

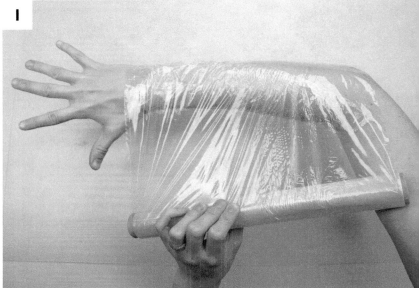

2 Tape Your Arm

Press the plastic wrap piece down securely to make sure it fits well around your arm. Grab a roll of duct tape. Instead of turning your arm into a tape tornado with one long strip, just tear off short tape pieces and place them evenly on all sides of your wrapped forearm. Try to avoid getting big wrinkles since they might distort your pattern.

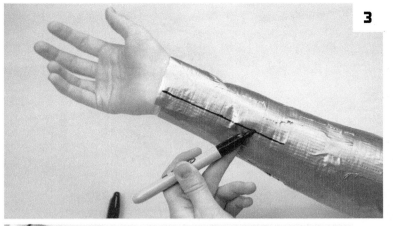

3 Mark the Centerline of the Pattern

Grab a marker and draw your desired bracer shape on the duct tape. It's a good idea to start with a middle line on the inner side of your forearm. Make a dot on the inner side of your wrist and one at the crook of your arm and simply connect both with a straight line.

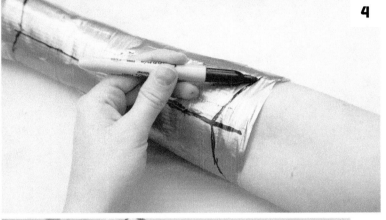

4 Shape the Pattern

Draw a half circle on your pattern at these two points to curve the edge. Try to keep both sides of your pattern as similar as possible. That way you'll get a nice, symmetrical bracer later.

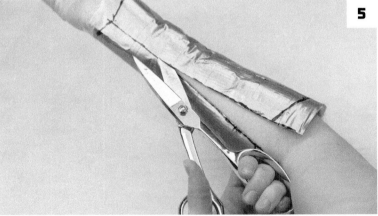

5 Cut the Pattern off Your Arm

Cutting yourself free might be tricky, so it's a good idea to call a friend or family member over to help. Ask them to cut you free very slowly and carefully! It helps to press a finger under the scissor blade and make slow and small cuts. We don't want any accidents here.

Try to resist the urge to shock your helper by shouting, "OUCH!" as soon as they touch you with the scissors.

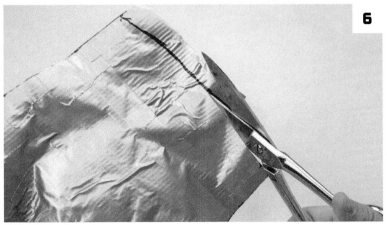

6 Trim the Edges

Once you're free from the wrap and tape, you can clean up your cutouts and trim the edges until you end up with a perfect copy of your forearm shape.

7 Flatten the Cut Pattern

To transform this into a usable bracer pattern, you'll have to transfer it to some regular flat paper. Stretch and flatten your cutout pattern to get rid of most of the wrinkles.

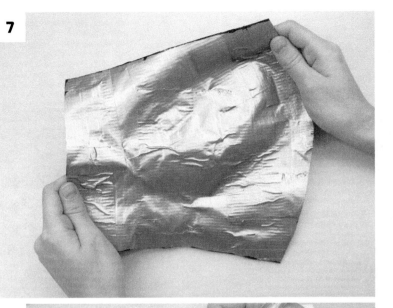

8 Trace the Pattern

Grab some thick paper and fold your sheet and your pattern template in the middle. Lay the folded pattern edge to the folded paper edge and start tracing all around the shape.

9 Cut the Paper Pattern

Cut around three sides of your drawing and unfold the paper. You'll have a perfectly symmetrical base for all of your upcoming bracers. This will now be your template for your very first bracer. You can use this for many more projects, so make sure not to throw it away. Store it in a pattern box until you need it again. It also helps to label what the pattern is. This bracer piece and many other following patterns will be a great resource for all your future costumes.

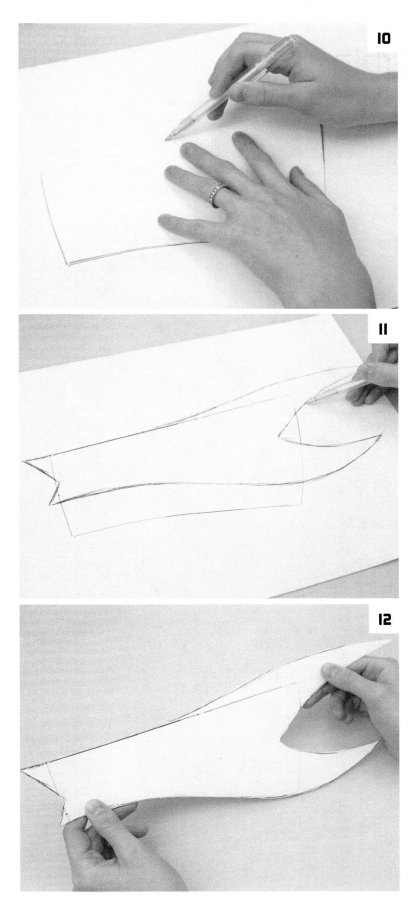

10 Trace the Base Design Again

While this pattern might already work for countless other costumes, every project will require a special size and shape. Adjusting it, however, is easy. For this specific example fold the paper bracer along the middle line and trace it onto a new piece of paper.

11 Adjust the Drawn Design

To get a pointy end and little spikes at the sides, draw on some new lines while using the basic shape as a foundation.

12 Cut the Final Pattern

If you want to have the final design open at the bottom, adjust the drawing in a way that does not go all the way around your forearm. The lines for the new bracer shape extend further than the original shape.

Cut everything out and hold it to your arm to get a feeling of the final shape. Finding the right size and shape can be quite tricky, especially for beginners. As you can see though, this step is really easy and fast. In no time you'll find the right solution. Adjusting patterns is much easier than adjusting the final costume piece, so take your time for this step!

Working with Worbla

After you've gotten a clean pattern, it's time to start crafting. As I mentioned in the material section of this book, Worbla gets as flexible as fabric once you've heated it up. It might also get bumpy and wrinkly, however, which is not good since we'll need a shiny and smooth armor for our costume. To gain a little more control over how the thermoplastic behaves in a heated state, it's necessary to stiffen it up a bit. If you've worked with fabric in the past, then you already know how inlays work. The same principle applies to Worbla even though we're using craft foam. So let's make a Worbla craft foam sandwich!

1 Transfer the Pattern to Foam

Transfer your pattern onto craft foam using a pen. We need two separate mirrored pieces for our bracer, so simply do this step twice and cut out both parts.

2 Transfer the Pattern to Worbla

Repeat the same step on Worbla, though this time you'll need much more material and will have to add ⅜" (1cm) more space around the edges.

Our sandwich will be Worbla, craft foam, Worbla, so we need two pieces of thermoplastic for every piece of foam. This applies for every costume piece you want to make with this technique. Your craft foam must be covered on both sides with Worbla. The result will be a super durable and nearly indestructible costume, just like real armor.

Cut out the Worbla pieces along your markings. You'll need a good pair of sharp scissors.

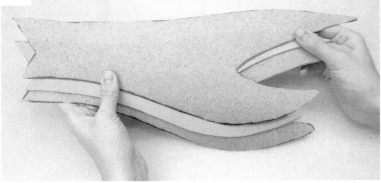

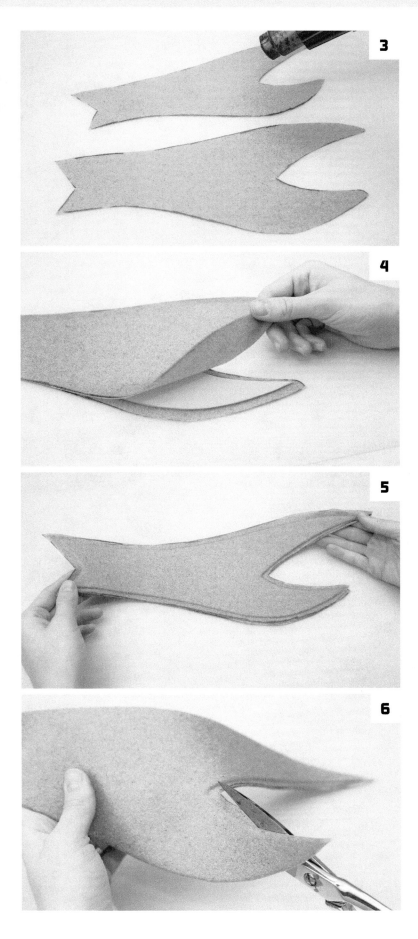

3 Heat up the Worbla

To activate Worbla's glue, you have to heat up the material evenly. It's best to do two parts at the same time so both parts have the same temperature.

Once heated up, Worbla might stick to your work surface, but you can avoid that. Baking paper is a cheap and great solution, though it gets destroyed after a few work steps. I prefer heat-resistant silicone mats. Just make sure the surface you work on doesn't contain any sort of plastic. It might melt or stick to the Worbla.

4 Sandwich the Worbla and Foam

Once your material has reached the right temperature, it will become slightly darker, shiny and sticky—that's the right point to turn off your heat gun, place your craft foam on top of one piece of Worbla and then cover the foam with the other Worbla piece.

5 Press the Pieces Together

Gently press all three layers together and use your thumb or the side of your scissors to trace and close all the edges around the foam core so it's sealed.

6 Trim Away the Extra

Once all the edges are sealed, carefully cut away the overlapping material without opening the edges again.

7 Press the Pieces Together

Repeat steps 2–6 for a mirrored piece. To activate the material's own glue, carefully heat up both pieces at the same time. Hold one of them in each hand and slowly press them together at the middle line. It might not be easy to mirror these pieces perfectly, so take your time and try not to tear open one end as you work towards the other.

8 Shape the Worbla

When you're done, it's finally time to form your bracer into the right shape. You'll get a nice result if you simply press your build directly over your arm. This only works as long as your material is still warm enough though. Don't worry, you can instantly cool down Worbla under cold water once you're happy with the shape. If you need a second try, simply use your heat gun again.

Another way to shape the Worbla is to slowly and carefully shape it with your hands. You can use both techniques for this bracer. Give it a simple form on your arm and shape the spiky tips with your fingertips. Then use your hands to shape the rest. If you are very heat sensitive, it helps to dip your fingertips into cold water—no need to burn yourself. Over time you may get used to the temperature.

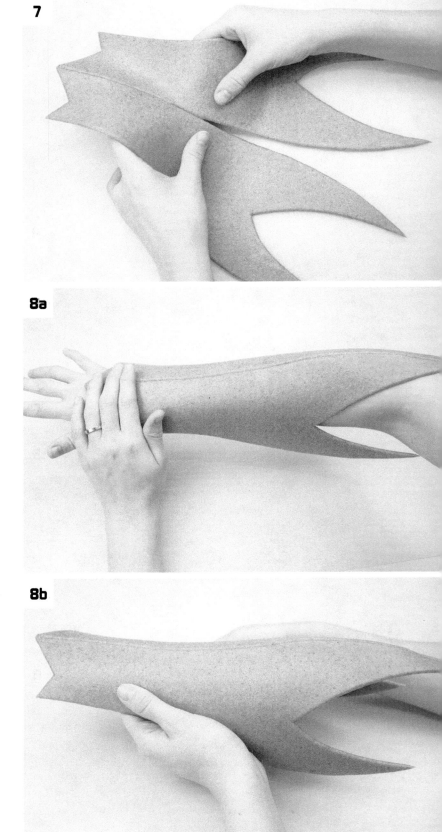

7

8a

8b

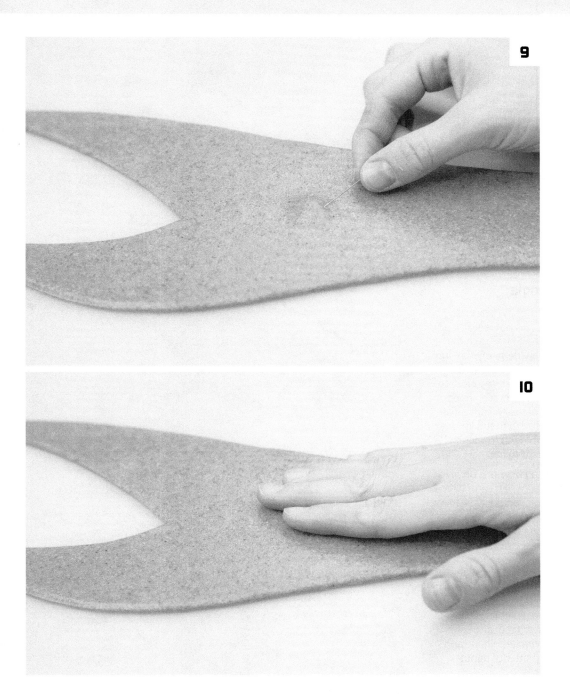

9 Get Rid of Heat Bubbles

As you may have noticed, you will need to reheat your Worbla quite a lot. Bending the material or simply heating it up a little bit too much or too fast will cause little air bubbles to be trapped between your craft foam and thermoplastic. It's simply air that expands between the layers of material. This might turn your shiny armor into a miniature hilly area full of annoying bumps. Doesn't really sound like armor, right?

Luckily there is an easy way to get rid of them. When the Worbla is still warm, stick a pin into the bubble and gently press all the air out.

10 Smooth out the Surface

With some additional pressure you can even let the tiny crater from the needle disappear until your surface looks perfect again. This is one of the reasons why I love Worbla so much as a crafting material. You can mess up as much as you want, but by simply reheating and reshaping your piece you can iron out your mistakes almost every time.

II Get the Perfect Angle

You may have noticed that the bracer I created for this example is not really supposed to be skintight. Since I built the pattern directly on the shape of my forearm, however, I will need to add an additional structure underneath this costume piece to lift it up a bit. I added a mini bracer inside my original design. It's basically just a small Worbla craft foam sandwich that is long enough to fit from one side to the other while covering my arm on the way.

Using this, the bracer can now rest on my forearm and stay at the angle I want. If you're not sure that your additional elements will fit, you can heat up a Worbla piece and stick it on with a little pressure to test it. Worbla will strongly bond to itself only when both parts are heated up at the same time. This test will let you rip off your attached piece again after it cools. Repeat this as many times as you want and use it for all kinds of experiments. Your armor smithing skills will improve dramatically over time, and soon you'll be able to just estimate a shape and bring it to life within a matter of minutes.

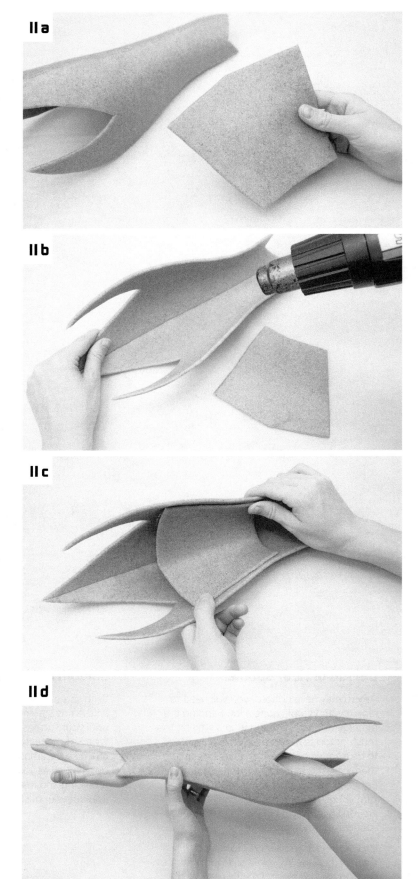

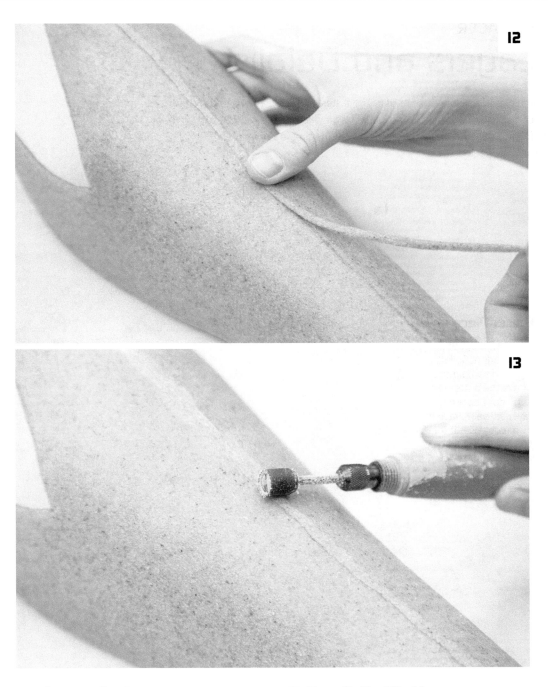

12

13

12 Clean up the Seam

Since this bracer consists of two separate mirrored pieces, it has a very visible seam in the middle. If you don't care about this little flaw, you can of course ignore it. If you want to get a perfect surface though, this simply will not do, but there is an easy way to get rid of the seam. All you need to do is cut a thin strip of double-layered Worbla. Heat up your bracer and your strip very carefully. Press the thin material over the seam with a good amount of pressure.

13 Smooth the Worbla

While the material is still hot, use your thumb or a tool to smooth it out as much as possible. Once it has cooled down, grab your Dremel, attach a standard sanding tip and sand all the way along the seam. Note that during your sanding work, tiny Worbla pieces and dust will fly everywhere, so don't forget to put on your safety glasses and respiratory protection. Carefully get rid of the raised edges and bring it all to the same height. The result should be a nice even surface without any sign of the hidden gap. Afterwards wash the dust and material leftovers away and dry your piece with a towel.

Adding Layers and Details

Adding more details is a technique all its own—luckily one that you can master quickly. Working with Worbla allows you to follow your own ideas and creativity and shape anything imaginable out of it. The fastest and easiest ways to get a few cool details are adding layers, edges and curves or swirls with some simple stripes.

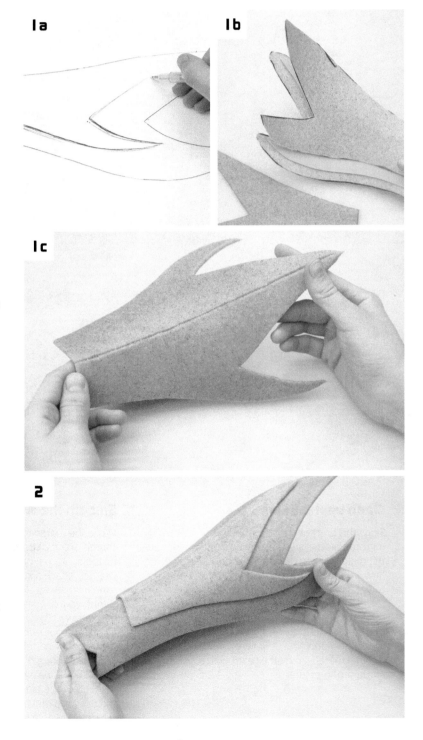

1a

1b

1c

2

1 Create a Smaller Bracer Piece

Flat armor pieces might do their job, but they can also look a little bit boring. So let's put on our 3-D glasses and add some more depth. Since we already have the pattern for our basic bracer shape, why not just use it to sketch an additional layer as well? Trace it on paper again and draw directly over it for a new pattern piece. By now you should be familiar with the process: Trace your shape onto craft foam and Worbla, heat the pieces up and sandwich them together to create the mini bracer.

2 Place the New Bracer Piece

After getting rid of any overlapping material, apply this new piece on top of your existing bracer by activating the glue with heat. Don't forget to close the center seam with your Dremel again.

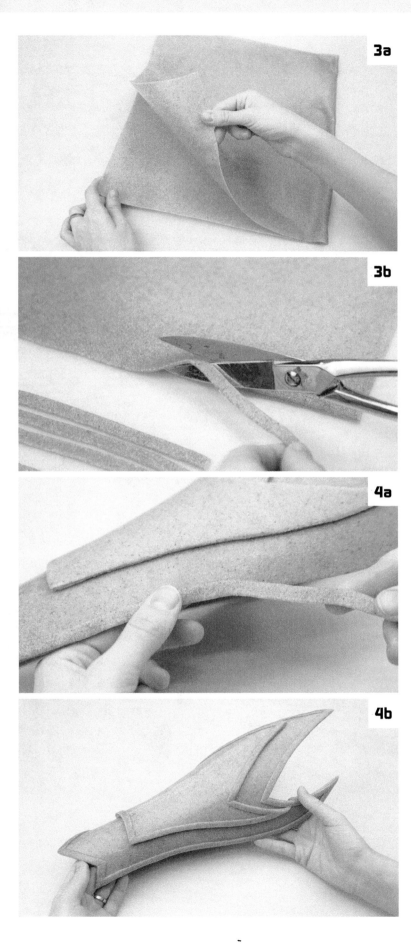

3 Cut Worbla Strips

One of my favorite techniques for details involves making strips out of double-layered Worbla. To make them you need to sacrifice some material though. Lay out a medium-sized sheet of Worbla on your table. Heat it up and fold it in half along the centerline. The folded size should be big enough to fit your entire bracer on it. Press your Worbla down and get rid of all the wrinkles, bumps and air bubbles.

Heat up your material again and start cutting it into strips of different widths. A sharp pair of scissors and a big table are a great help here; however, it might also be a good idea to mark your lines in advance. Don't worry if your lines don't turn out perfectly straight or if they vary in thickness—it's not an exact science and it will not really matter later anyway. Worbla is a lot easier to cut when hot, so you might want to reheat it every once in a while.

4 Add the Strips to the Bracer

Once you're done cutting, heat up the strip as well as the area where you want to place this additional element on your bracer. If both parts are slightly sticky, simply press your strip on and cut it off at the end. The side of your scissors will be helpful to bring the strip into shape afterwards.

Work around the main parts of your armor piece and add more strips to give your edges a little more oomph.

5 Keep Your Scraps

Working with thermoplastics, you'll end up with a ton of leftover scraps. You may wonder if you have to throw them all away or if there is something you can still do with them. Good news! Worbla scraps can be squished together and used like a thick clay. You can sculpt spikes, twirls and all kinds of neat details. Grab some leftovers, heat them up and start squeezing them together.

Once the material is evenly heated, you can start rolling it around and build what you want out of it. Be careful not to burn your fingers. Keep using cold water to cool down your skin or simply work with heat-protective gloves.

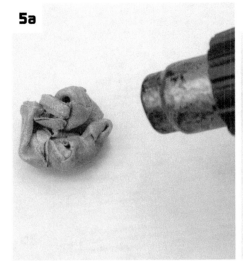

6 Mold the Scraps

For nice raised twirls, roll your leftovers until you get a cute little Worbla snake. Cut it into smaller pieces. Pinch the ends until they are pointy and shape the snake between your thumb and index finger. This should create a triangle form that you can then twist and stick to your bracer.

This step takes a little bit more time since the Worbla needs to be heated all the way through, so don't lose your patience. Use the heat gun every few minutes; otherwise the scraps will cool in the center and will be a lot tougher to heat up again.

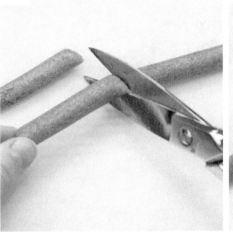

7 Add Gems

For this example, I added two shiny resin gemstones for detail. I attached them with hot glue and then created the gemstone setting by gluing a strip of Worbla around it. You can make gems yourself by casting them out of clear resin or buying some at your local hobby store.

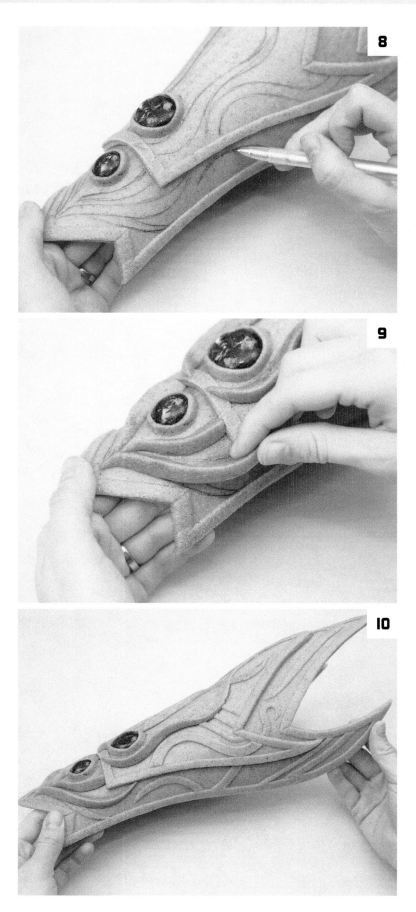

8 Map out Your Design

If your details are elaborate, it's a good idea to draw them on before. This helps for mirrored designs. It's totally fine to make mistakes with your pen, but it will be hard to get rid of glued-on details. This will also make sure you won't forget even the tiniest piece.

9 Attach Worbla Details

Attach the little Worbla snakes you created as well as a couple of additional strips, and your piece will already look a lot more interesting. Heat the Worbla strips and the bracer to activate the glue and press them down firmly.

10 Complete the Detail Placement

Keep adding details until you're satisfied. With just scissors and a heat gun you are able to create everything you can imagine from this stuff. It's forgiving, very flexible and needs only a few tools to get shaped. Additionally, the final result will be so durable that even your grandkids can wear your old costumes later.

Priming and Painting

While Worbla is an awesome crafting material, it does have one disadvantage: its rough surface texture. If you were to paint the material in its natural state, it would look like you had applied color to sandpaper. This might be what you're looking for in some cases, but usually we want bracers to be smooth and shiny. So, let's prime this piece and prepare it for the upcoming paint job.

For the paint job, simple acrylics and brushes are just fine. Find products with high viscosity and good pigmentation. If the colors are too fluid, you might have to apply the color coat up to ten times until your piece is fully covered. Not only is this a waste of time, but it can be frustrating as well. So don't try to save when it comes to paint quality!

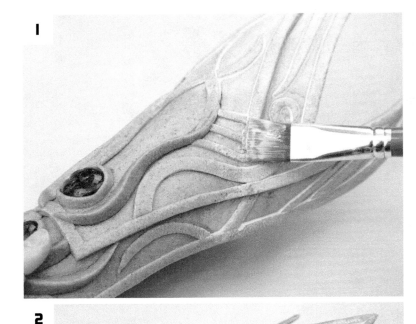

1 Thin the Glue and Apply

There are a couple of different primers you can use to give your Worbla a much smoother surface. My current favorite is regular white glue or wood glue. I tried Elmer's white glue and it works just fine. Thin your glue with a bit of water and simply paint it on with a big brush.

2 Coat the Whole Surface

Try to use a minimum of glue to avoid visible drops on your armor piece. Every coat needs to dry before you can apply a new one, so wait a bit or speed up the process by using a hair dryer.

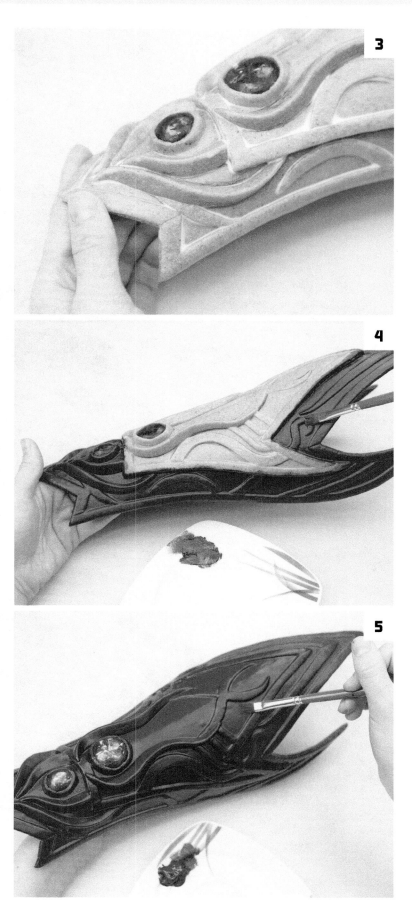

3 Let the Glue Dry, Then Add More

Don't rush this step or you will get cracks in your glue coat. It needs to dry out slowly and evenly. Depending on how thick you applied your glue primer and how smooth you want your surface to be, something between five and seven layers of glue should do the trick. I find priming to be the most boring step of creating a costume or prop. For a nice and smooth finish it needs to be done, though.

4 Apply the Base Color

When painting costume pieces, I usually go from dark to bright, so I always pick the darkest shade of the color first. The base of the bracer had to be gold, so I started with a dark brown. I covered the entire larger bracer with paint as well as the underside of the piece.

5 Paint the Middle Piece

The middle piece had to be bright purple, so I used a dark shade of this color first. At this point, it's totally fine to buy a basic acrylic and mix it with a little bit of black. Don't mix too little, though. It's hard to match the exact same shade again if you run out of paint. Put your color in a tube or in your refrigerator if you want to use it later.

6 Create a Gradient of Color

For this step you'll need your main color shade; in this example it's a bright purple. Usually getting a nice, smooth gradient requires a lot of mixing and smudging, but there is an easier way called "drybrushing." Simply dip the tip of your brush very slightly into the paint, and then clean it with some tissue paper. Don't use any water—it's called drybrushing for a reason. Dab on your armor piece from the center outwards to get a very soft paint application. The more you dab on the same spot, the brighter your paint job will be.

Do this on all the areas between your swirls, lines and details. This creates natural looking shadows around all the shapes that you built up before. If you want, you can apply another even brighter layer to make your highlights pop more.

7 Paint with Gold

Next, I repeated the gradient for the golden parts as well. I dipped my brush slightly into golden acrylic and dabbed carefully between all the swirls. Apply additional paint mostly in the center and dab in a smooth circle. This way all the borders will stay dark, and you'll get a nice antique-looking metallic effect.

With that much dabbing, your brush will be worn out pretty quickly, so get a fresh one. You still have to paint all the swirls and details. Since you don't need any shading here, directly dip your brush in paint and turn all those details golden as well. Metallic acrylics usually don't cover that well, so you might need to go over the same spot twice. Maybe add a little bit of white to save some time. Good alternatives are products from Rub'n Buff or special metallic-effect paints.

6

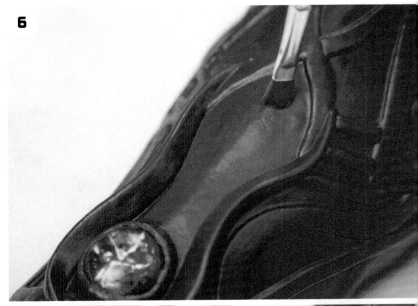

7a

7b

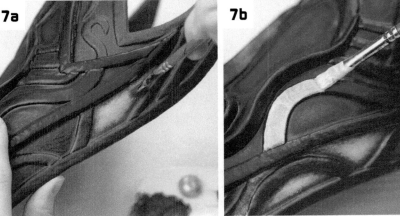

7c

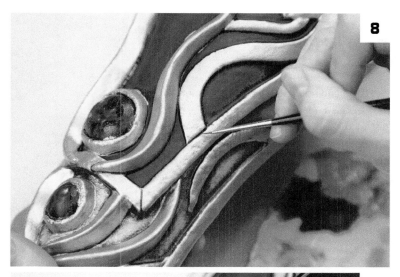

8 Outline the Edges

The result looked nice already, but I wasn't quite done yet. Painting, especially dabbing and drybrushing, never turns out perfectly clean, so you will need to fix a few spots and unwanted brushstrokes here and there. Grab a fine brush, dip it into your original base color (dark brown or dark purple) and trace fine lines around all the shapes, applications and details. It's totally up to you how thick you want your lines to be and how much paint you want to apply, but you'll notice this step will give your piece a really nice effect.

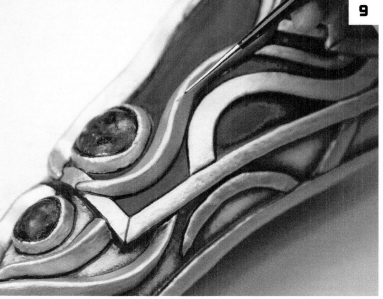

9 Add Highlights

Just like with your dark colors you can add bright highlights pretty much the same way. Pick pure white or mix it with your golden acrylic to get a shiny version of your detail color. Paint some of the borders of your details to create edges that look like they're reflecting sunlight. This will make your build look even sharper.

These steps are optional, and it all comes down to personal preference. The end result will not look like a real metal armor piece, but more cartoonish and hand painted. It's a lot of extra work, but I think it pays off most of the time. If you're striving to highlight every detail of your costume and give it this special high-definition look, it's surely a great technique for you.

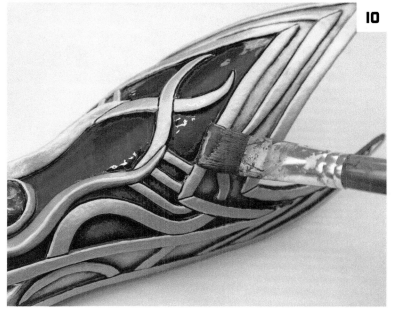

10 Seal the Color

You'll need to protect your beautiful paint job from scratches and bad weather. While you are wearing the costume, armor pieces might rub against each other and scratch away your paint. The color on your Worbla is only a very thin layer of acrylics, and damage might happen faster than you can imagine. There is an easy way to prevent this. All you need is a good clear varnish from your local hardware store. I usually prefer a brush-on product with a medium satin shine effect, though there are also countless spray solutions. Glossy finishes can make your elaborately painted armor look like cheap plastic, so it's best to avoid those. A satin or matte finish is perfect for something that should look like metal, wood or leather. Always consider which material you want to imitate before you apply your varnish.

Attachment with D-Rings

Finally, your new bracer is done and you're ready to head out to the next convention to show it to everybody, right? Well, not quite—you still need to make sure it's attached properly to your body. As always there are tons of ways to accomplish this. You can work with magnets, rucksack buckles, Velcro tape or leather strips—just don't go out there and hot glue the bracers to your skin! A well-planned attachment is comfortable, easy to get into and gives you enough movement while preventing your costume from falling apart at the convention. It's a nice addition if your solution is nearly invisible or looks authentic enough to give your armor pieces that extra accurate look.

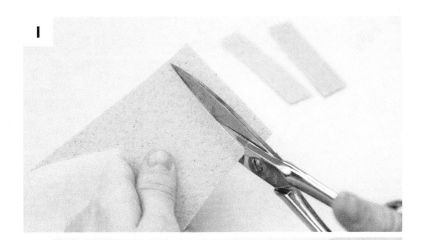

1 Cut Worbla Strips

Cut out short strips of Worbla that are small enough to fit through a metal D-ring. Always save your scraps! Scrap Worbla pieces are perfect for small parts like this.

2 Attach the Worbla to the D-Ring

Smaller D-rings are good for bracers and larger ones are good for breastplates or leg armor. You can get them in many different shapes and colors, so choose the ones that best fit your costume. Heat the Worbla strips and close them around the straight end of the ring to get a nice base for your bracer attachment.

3 Make a Cut for the Attachment

Try to plan in advance how many rings you will need to hold the armor piece gently to your body while not giving it too much space to move around. Heat up a spot where you want to put the ring on the inner side of your armor piece and make a small cut right to the foam core. It's important to use your heat gun only on this small area so the rest of your costume piece stays in shape.

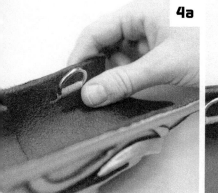
4a

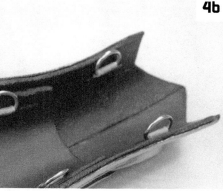
4b

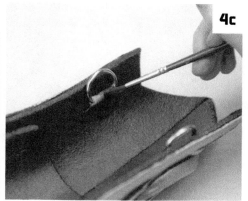
4c

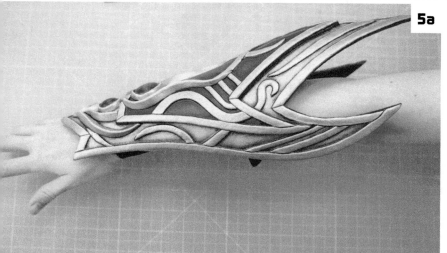
5a

4 Add the Attachments to the Bracer

Carefully slide the cold Worbla part of your D-ring attachment into the cut. Use your heat gun again and close the hole with some pressure. After this area has cooled down, you'll have a pretty much indestructible base for all kinds of attachments.

Repeat this step a few times around the edges. As you can see, I decided to use six D-rings in total, three on each side of my bracer. To hide the Worbla under the D-rings, you can paint them black so they blend in.

5 Lace a Strap Through the Rings

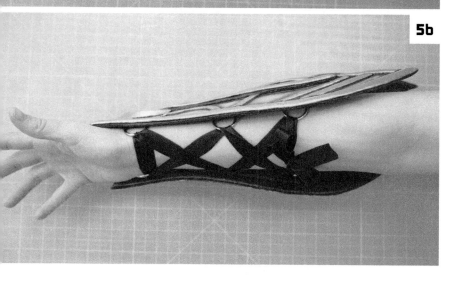
5b

Now you have a few handy rings that can hold the bracer on your arm. You can use rubber bands, strings, leather straps, Velcro tape or any other material for this. Just pick something you like that fits your costume. You can even sew a cool leather belt system. This solution takes only a few minutes and can always be upgraded or changed later if you want. For this bracer I used a simple black satin ribbon that can slide through all the rings and over my arm. A band is enough to hold the bracer in place and looks elegant enough for a real wizard.

Diablo III Wizard

One of my favorite costumes is the Wizard from the video game *Diablo III*. Usually my projects are either very focused on armor making or on sewing. This project, however, allowed me to combine both approaches to bring this magical dream of purple and gold to life. If you take a closer look, you'll notice that the fabric part was quite simple: A black waist cincher and a few dozen layers of white, black and purple dupioni silk for the open skirt. The armor parts took quite some time and effort though. All the tiny details, swirls and ornaments drove me crazy after a while, but the result was worth it. Since I wanted to get a very durable costume, Worbla was my choice for the armor. Even the staff was mostly built out of this material with a bit of EVA foam as a core. The final costume turned out to be really comfy, and I still wear it as often as I can.

Materials

- EVA foam (2mm, 5mm)

Paints and Glues

- Acrylic paints
- Brush cleaner or turpentine substitute
- Contact cement
- Gold chrome spray paint
- Liquid Plasti Dip
- Varnish

Tools

- Assorted brushes
- Black marker
- Craft knife or box cutter
- Dremel
- Dust mask and safety glasses
- Heat gun
- Hot glue gun and sticks
- Pen and paper
- Scissors
- Water-soluble pen or chalk

Miscellaneous

- D-rings and furniture leather
- Duct tape
- Plastic wrap
- Spherical piece of plastic, metal or pottery
- Velcro

How to Create a Breastplate

An essential piece that you will probably need for most of your armor costume projects is a breastplate. A big percentage of fictional characters from all kinds of video games, fantasy movies or comic books wear these bulky protectors. They come in all kinds of crazy shapes and designs. Creating such an elaborate piece might seem intimidating at first, but I am going to show you a couple of tricks to create comfortable and eye-catching breastplates. Since we worked with Worbla for our last example, it's a good time to introduce you to our other main costume crafting material: EVA foam.

EVA foam is a lot lighter, softer and more flexible than its thermoplastic counterpart. It is also a lot cheaper, so it might be a good alternative if you're working with a tight budget. Just be aware that you will have to reinforce your finished piece since foam cracks and tears a lot faster. Also be careful when building full body armor costumes; since foam insulates heat, you will sweat like crazy in the sun.

So let's get started with the next armor piece. What better example could there be than a mighty Wonder Woman breastplate!

Creating a Pattern

I already showed you my basic technique for pattern making with my bracer tutorial. The same principle applies here, so let's keep this part a bit shorter. To create a fitted breastplate pattern, put on a skintight shirt as a base. If you're a girl, it's also good to wear the same bra you intend to wear with your finished costume later on. This will guarantee a perfect fit.

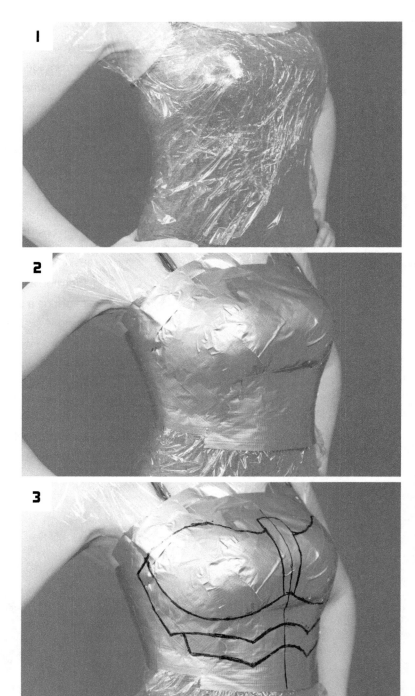

1 Create a Plastic Wrap Base

It's best to get a friend or family member to help you out with the next steps. Cover the area of your armor piece in plastic wrap. Make sure to extend the plastic wrap farther than where your final pattern shape will be and press down on the plastic wrap to make it smooth and tight.

2 Add Duct Tape

Slowly and deliberately add little strips of duct tape until you're covered completely. Try to keep the wrinkles and bumps in the tape to a minimum. Depending on the shape of your reference design, you may have to cover your whole torso from your neck to your hips and all around the front and back. In this case, though, you only need the area around your ribs. The Wonder Woman piece I built here has a very distinctive design where the breastplate covers only the front of the chest, so I applied the tape over that area while leaving the back open.

3 Draw Your Design

Once you've added your layer of duct tape, grab a black marker and draw a middle line for your breastplate. For larger pieces, I recommend adding more lines to the back and on the sides under your armpits as well. You can even draw on a full muscular structure to get a better orientation of the right shape for your armor piece. In this case, however, it's pretty simple, so I just drew the basic outlines.

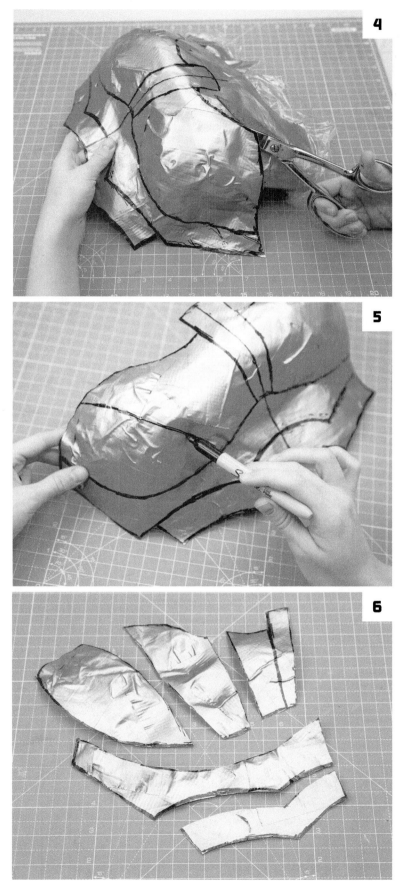

4 Cut the Pattern off Yourself

Cut yourself free (or have a friend help) on one of the sides or your back and trim away any tape you don't need. You should now have a perfect copy of your torso. To be honest, it's a lot easier to do this on a male body. Having breasts makes costume crafting much more complicated!

5 Draw Additional Pattern Curves

While drawing patterns with additional curves might already be complicated, creating round shapes out of flat foam pieces is even more tricky. Just like a blouse or a dress often has a seam in the middle of the cups, you must add these additional cutting lines to your pattern. Otherwise their round shape will make it hard to get a clean pattern.

6 Cut the Pattern

Cut everything out and you should be able to lay down all the pieces without too many wrinkles. Just like last time, if you keep everything clean and symmetrical, you'll need only one half of your breastplate pattern. That way all of your pieces will have the same size and shape.

Working with EVA Foam

It's time to grab some material. For this example, I used 5mm sheets of dense gray EVA foam. It's the perfect thickness for a thin base layer of armor that you can then easily add more details to. Additionally, it's dense enough to keep even a thin layer of material solid and durable.

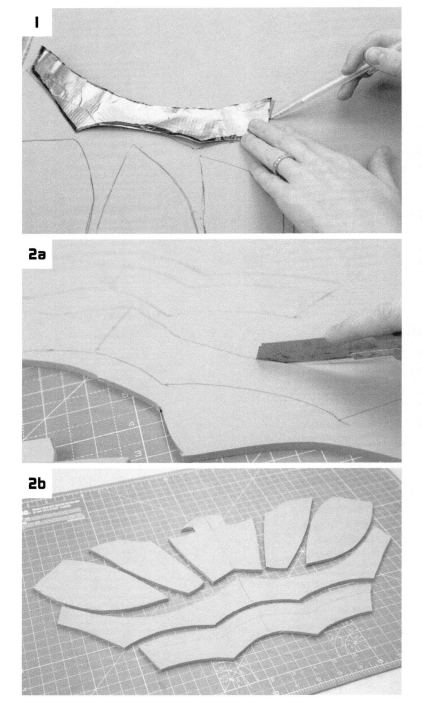

1 Trace the Pattern onto Foam

Since you're going to mirror your patterns, you will have to trace them twice onto your material. As you can see I skipped the part where I transfer my rough tape patterns to a clean piece of paper. If your shapes are clean enough, you're fine with just using the tape template on the EVA foam.

2 Cut out the Pieces

Think about what pieces you will need twice and which parts got cut in half through the middle line. You can transfer them right next to each other at their mirror edge and cut them out in one big piece. This not only saves you from doing unnecessary work, but it also makes your costume piece more durable. Use a sharpened box cutter or craft knife and try to get through the foam in one clean, straight cut.

Extend those pattern parts that you know will overlap each other. In this example I had to enlarge the bottom part a bit since I knew it had to be glued to the backside of the piece that comes on top.

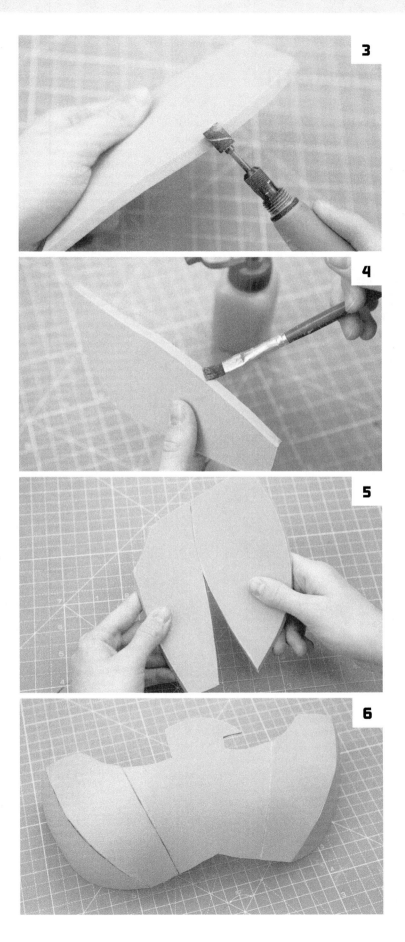

3 Sand the Edges

Before you start gluing together this little breastplate puzzle, first think about which parts will end up getting rounded. To avoid nasty bumps and cutting lines, it's useful to sand the edges depending on the angle you want to glue those parts together in. With a little bit of sanding work you'll get a nice and almost invisible seam. Use your rotary tool to create a slight bevel all around those edges.

4 Add Glue

Apply a thin layer of contact cement to both sides and let them dry for a bit.

I keep my glue in a little bottle. Contact cement usually comes in big metal cans and is cumbersome to work with in those containers. After opening a new can I simply pour some fresh glue in these little sealed plastic bottles that I bought. That way I don't need to worry about dried out and clumpy adhesive, and I always get the perfect amount of glue for my projects.

5 Press the Pieces Together

A few moments after applying the glue, press the pieces together very carefully. Once your glue has dried enough, you'll get a connection that will hold through countless conventions.

6 Assemble More Pieces

Put together more of the breastplate using the same method. As you can see with the right angles, this armor part already looks pretty rounded.

Heat Shaping with Foam

Once you've glued all of your pieces together, you'll see that the shape is still pretty angular. This always happens when you work with flat foam sheets, so don't worry. Now our heat-shaping technique comes in to play. Heat your material up, pull it over something or shape it by hand, and enjoy the result. With just a little bit of heat, you're able to create nicely rounded helmets, breastplates, shoulder armor and much more. Just try it out!

1 Find a Round Piece for Molding

The bust of the breastplate needs to be rounded, and all you need for that is a spherical piece of plastic, metal or pottery in the right cup size. I usually use a translucent acrylic sphere for this job.

2 Heat up the Foam

Heat up your foam breastplate from both sides until it gets noticeably softer and more flexible.

3 Shape the Warm Foam

Drag the warm foam area over the sphere with some pressure. Only release it after it has cooled down again. You'll notice that your foam shape holds the form and has become beautifully round.

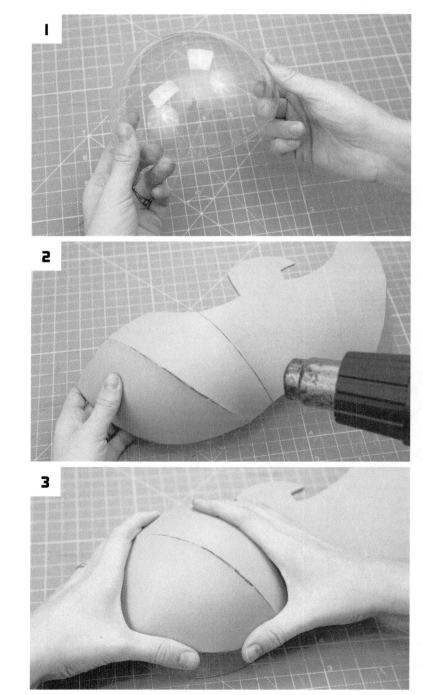

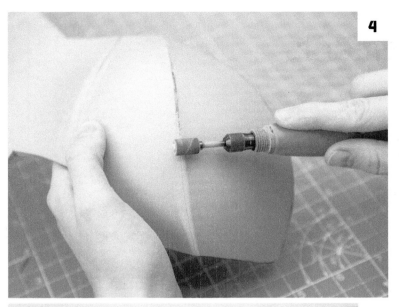

4 Sand the Seams

To get rid of any overlapping material, unwanted edges and glue leftovers, use your Dremel or sandpaper. Clean up the foam seam by carefully dremeling it all the way down. Handling Worbla seams is very similar, though you need a lot less force to carve away material. Be careful not to dig too deep.

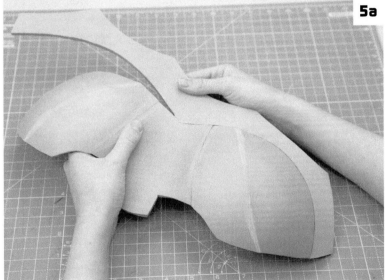

5 Assemble Additional Pieces

Once the breast area is curved, you can glue on the other foam parts. It's easier to clean your build before assembling it. Afterward, it might be hard to reach a special area once everything is fixed together. Make sure to sand in a well-ventilated area in combination with good respiratory protection. You don't want to get all the nasty foam dust in your lungs.

As you can see, creating the basic shape and adding layers to it works very similarly to Worbla. You just need extra glue to connect your pieces. It's important to understand the techniques first and foremost since you can then change what material you want to use based on the project.

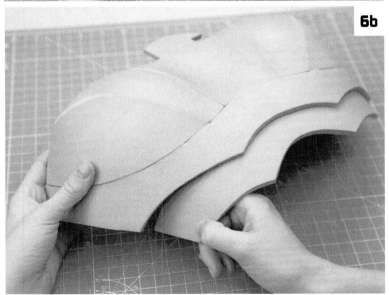

Details and Ornaments

Now it's finally time to add some details. The design might look complicated, but in fact this part is super simple. Just like with Worbla, you can simply cut a few strips out of craft foam or EVA foam.

1 Cut Strips and Shapes for Details

I used 2mm thick sheets for this since I did not want my details to stand out too much. They are pretty easy to cut and create a slightly raised effect to give your armor piece more depth and interesting highlights. Cut multiple foam strips of the same width.

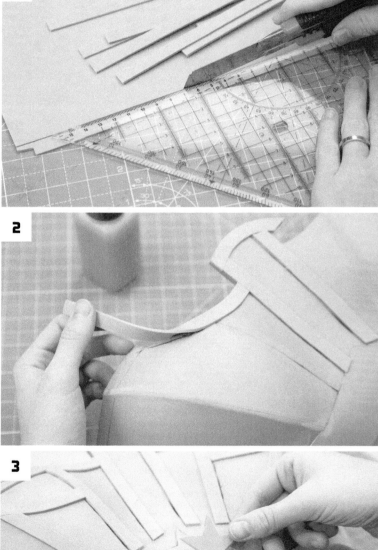

2 Start Adding Detail Pieces

It's always a good idea to plan where you want to add further elements. Remember, you need to cover both parts in glue—your strips as well as the breastplate, so it's important to set markings in advance. Just grab a pen, draw where you want to place your lines and fill this area and the back of your strips with a thin layer of contact cement. After you've waited a moment for the glue to set, press the strips onto your marked areas.

3 Place the Final Detail Pieces

Keep layering on the strips of foam until you're satisfied with the design. In addition to thin strips, I added a few thicker ones and some patriotic stars to really nail Wonder Woman's typical design. This should really do justice to the original reference artwork.

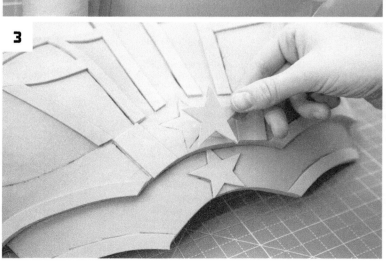

Priming with Plasti Dip

To keep this book as diverse and helpful as possible, I want to show you a number of different products you can choose from. So this time let me introduce you to a new primer that works great in combination with foam. Mainly used in the automotive industry, the rubber coating Plasti Dip is available as a brush-on or spray version. For this example I'm going with the brush-on product. It has a very creamy viscosity similar to acrylics. You can also get it in different colors, but I find plain black to be the most useful. As an alternative you can work with latex, a prodcut called Rosco Flexbond and other rubber-like primers.

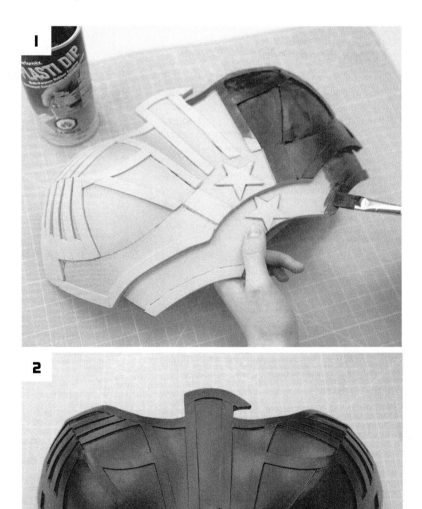

1 Start Priming the Foam

It's best to prime a small test square of foam first to familiarize yourself with the process. Plasti Dip is not that hard to handle properly, and you'll get used to it in no time.

For a proper application dip your brush into the can and spread a thin coat of rubber on your foam. Plasti Dip dries pretty quickly and it might be tricky to get a clean, bumpless layer. It helps to apply a thin and quick coat first. You don't need your first layer to totally cover since you have to repeat this step a few times anyway.

2 Finish Priming

To get a strong and thick rubber coat, add at least two to three layers. When you notice that the rubber starts hardening on your brush, you can always clean it with a brush cleaner or turpentine substitute.

Finish covering the rest of the breastplate. The final result will be a nice, flexible rubber skin for your foam. This will protect your build while still allowing it to twist and bend. Additionally your armor piece is more durable and now has a perfect base for the upcoming paint job.

Spray Paint and Acrylics

Since Wonder Woman protects the innocent and defeats evil, she needs really shiny golden armor. Instead of swinging my brush though, I wanted to show how handy spray paint can be. Even though you could just use regular acrylics like you saw in my previous example, it's easier to get a super reflective metallic color coat with spray paint. While you would have to apply two to three coats of brush-on acrylics to get a nice covering layer, the same can be achieved with spray paint within a few seconds. Just don't forget to go to a well-ventilated area and use respiratory protection. Fumes from spray cans are toxic and sometimes flammable, so always consider this.

1 Apply Spray Paint

For this example I went with a chrome gold spray paint from the hardware store. Make sure to read the instructions on the product before you use it. Shake the can and apply a thin base layer. It can be hard to reach all the spots and edges, so spray from every angle as you go around your piece. Some sprays might need to be handled differently. Usually you need to apply a thin and even coat from a distance of around 8" (20cm) and let it dry for a few minutes.

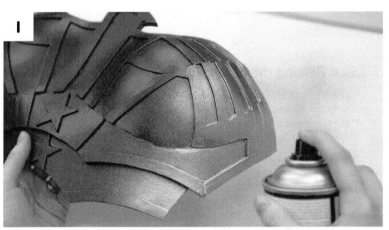

2 Cover the Whole Breastplate

Continue spraying the breastplate evenly to cover all the foam. The result will be a lovely metallic paint without any brushstrokes or blemishes.

3 Add Dark Shadows

It's time to add gradients. Work from dark to bright. Paint all the areas where you want to have shadows in a dark color. Mix together some brown and black acrylic paint and start to brush directly on the dried spray paint, leaving the edge lines gold.

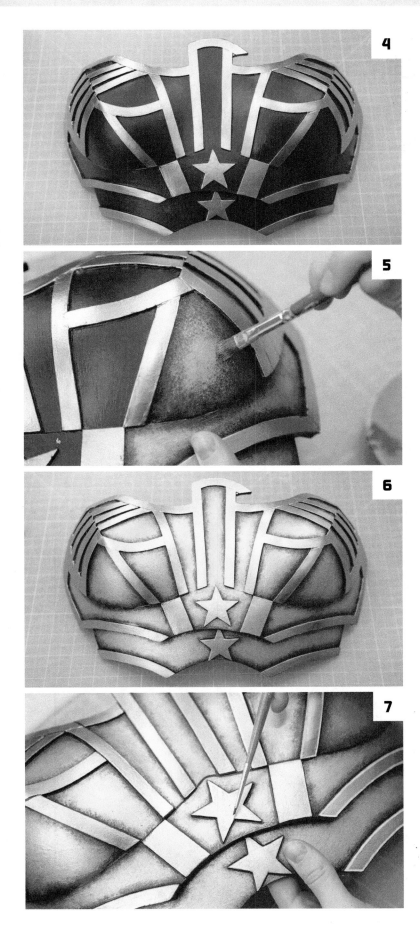

4 Fill the Rest of the Shadows

Continue to fill in the darker spaces with the acrylic paint. After you're done you'll have shiny reflective golden lines and some very dark spaces.

5 Add Shading

Grab a medium-sized flat brush and dip it into high-pigmented gold acrylic. Just like with the bracer, start to dab color to the darker areas. It's important to start applying color in the center first and then work your way to the edges. The more you dab, the less color will be on your brush and the shading will come naturally. This makes the golden color look more used and old. Wonder Woman has seen some battles after all, so her armor would not be super shiny and new. You can also use your brush with spray paint. Spray the color into a little puddle and dip your brush in it. Spray paints are not water based, though, and you'll need a special brush cleaner to reuse the brush afterwards.

6 Finish Shading

Keep working around the breastplate and add shading in all the dark spots. After you're done, use a thin brush to add brown lines around the golden edges. This helps not only to clean up any messed-up brush dabs but also to define clear shapes.

7 Add Highlights

Paint white lines on the golden borders. This step helps the details pop out even more.

I really like to add these little highlights, and I think they help a lot to make your piece look interesting even from afar. It's of course completely up to you if you do this step or not. You'll also find more examples later in this book with more realistic paint jobs.

Finally, don't forget to apply a coat of varnish to protect your work.

Breastplate Attachments

Let's move on to the next part: attaching the breastplate. People tend to forget that this is actually a very crucial part of costume making. After spending weeks creating armor, you don't just want to hot glue it to your body, right? I already showed you how to handle D-rings in the last example, and the same basic principle applies here. This time, though, we're going a little bit further and doing it with EVA foam. Instead of a Worbla piece and a satin ribbon I'm going to use strips of furniture leather. This heavy fabric looks very natural and is available in many different colors. Attachments made with it often fit better on a costume than regular cloth or strings. Furthermore, it's a very durable material and doesn't stretch—perfect for armor attachments.

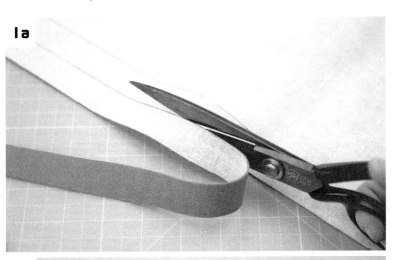

1a

I Cut and Assemble Your Attachments

Choose a medium-sized D-ring and cut out long leather strips in a width that fits through your metal ring. These belts will need to wrap around your torso for the attachment of your breastplate, so make sure they are long enough.

Afterwards cut a few pieces that easily fit around your D-ring. 3" (8cm) was just fine for me. Now add some hot glue at one end, drag your piece through the ring and press both edges together.

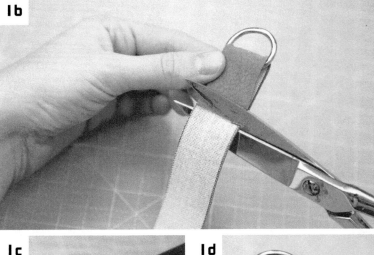

1b

1c

1d

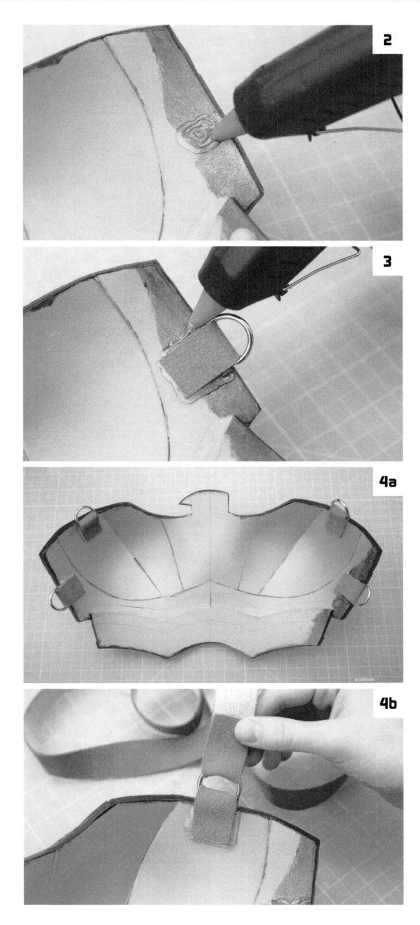

2 Decide Your Placement

Consider where you want to put your D-rings next. Your attachment should allow you enough movement while fitting tightly at the same time. There is no right or wrong way to do this; the most important thing is to make your costume as comfortable as you can. It's a good idea to hold your armor piece to your body and then think about how you need to mount it. When you have decided the placement, go ahead and add a good amount of hot glue to the spot where you want to place your first D-ring.

3 Attach the D-Rings

While the glue is still hot, press on the leather of your D-ring piece. You can also reinforce your connection by adding more glue around the edge.

4 Adhere All the Rings and Attach the Straps

I decided to place a ring on the top and the outer side of each of my bust cups. Now you need two very long strips of furniture leather. Pull one end of it through the metal ring and use more hot glue to keep it there. For this example I needed to permanently attach them only at the top rings. The strap will be laced through the other lower ring.

5 Test the Fit

For a proper and comfortable belt system you need a final fitting test. Place your breastplate on your body and pull your straps through the D-rings. Basically the attachment works a little bit like a bra—you'll need belts that go from the tops of your cups over your shoulders. Additionally, they need to go under your arms to the bottom D-rings on the other side and then connect at your back. Your breastplate should stay close to your chest, not too low or too high.

Bear in mind that during the fitting test, you should wear the same underwear that you want to wear with the final costume. If you forget your undersuit, shapewear or simply wear the wrong bra, your breastplate might not fit perfectly later on.

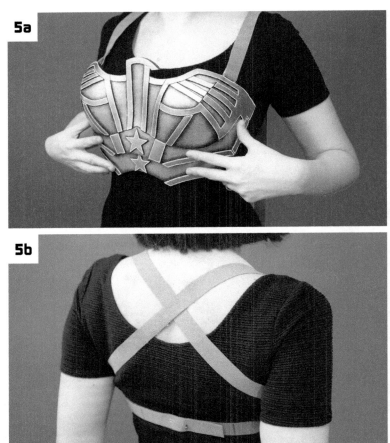

6 Mark the Placement

Cut off the straps so they roughly end at your back where they overlap. Mark how long the straps need to be so you know where to place Velcro. Use a water-soluble pen to highlight the area around your spine. Regular chalk works fine as well.

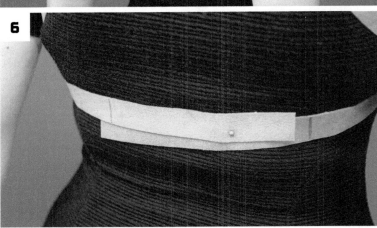

7 Add Velcro

Take your breastplate off and generously hot glue Velcro to the marked areas, one side to the back and the other side to the front of the furniture leather so they'll match up and stick together. It's always good to make your Velcro a little bit longer so you can widen or tighten your attachment as needed. Congratulations! Your breastplate attachment is now done!

DC Comics Wonder Woman

I absolutely love Wonder Woman, and when I saw this armored version of her in the concept art for the video game *Injustice,* I knew I had to make this costume. My reference, however, was only a blurry picture from the Internet, so I had to be quite creative to find clear lines and shapes. The entire armor set was made out of Worbla, but you can also use EVA foam instead. For the undersuit I sewed together a simple swimsuit body with some thigh highs and arm warmers. A dense black wig and a bit of makeup made the whole costume complete.

Photo by Darshelle Stevens: darshellestevens.com

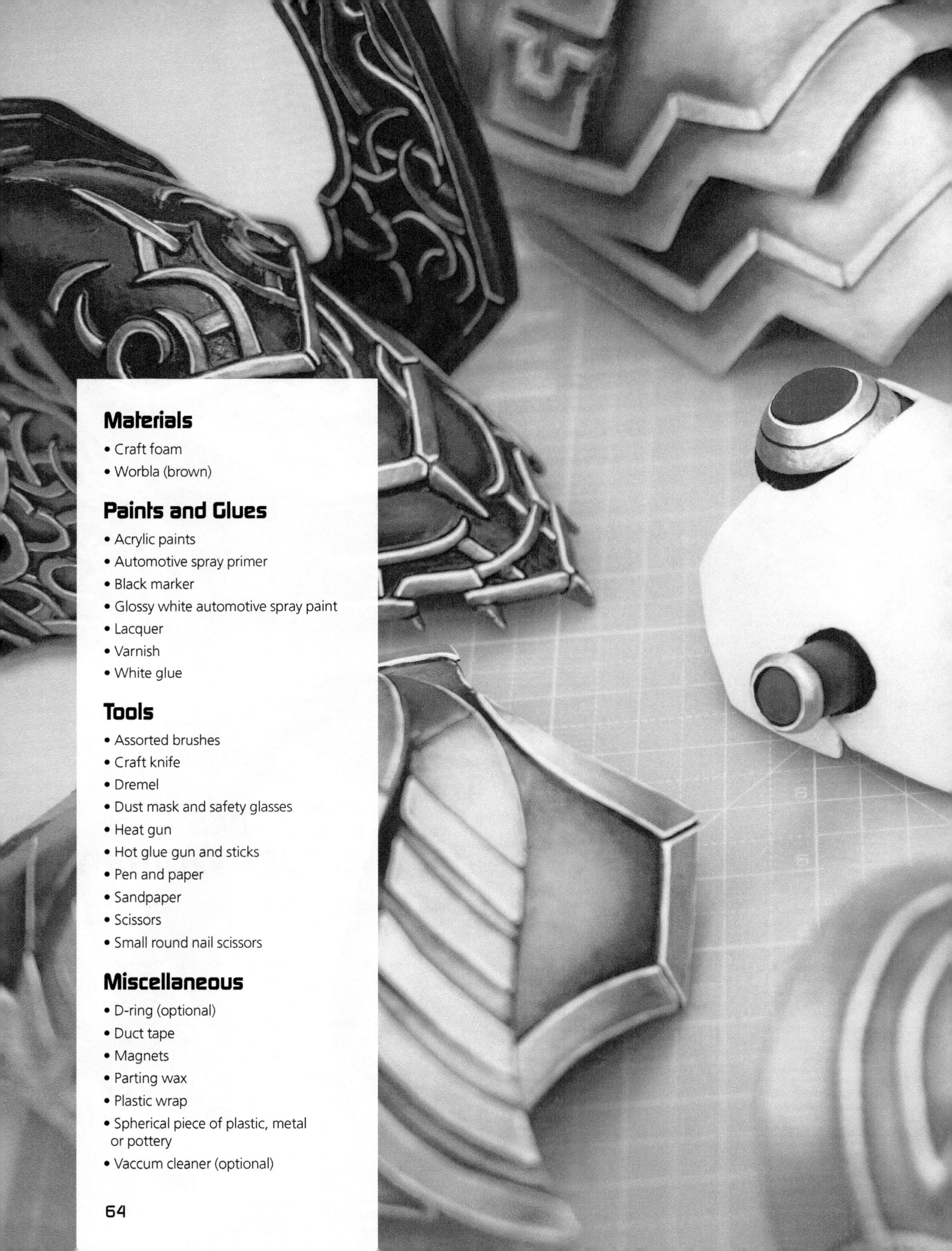

Materials

- Craft foam
- Worbla (brown)

Paints and Glues

- Acrylic paints
- Automotive spray primer
- Black marker
- Glossy white automotive spray paint
- Lacquer
- Varnish
- White glue

Tools

- Assorted brushes
- Craft knife
- Dremel
- Dust mask and safety glasses
- Heat gun
- Hot glue gun and sticks
- Pen and paper
- Sandpaper
- Scissors
- Small round nail scissors

Miscellaneous

- D-ring (optional)
- Duct tape
- Magnets
- Parting wax
- Plastic wrap
- Spherical piece of plastic, metal or pottery
- Vaccum cleaner (optional)

How to Create a Pauldron

Shoulder pieces are pretty common for many different costume designs, but their weird rounded shapes often make crafting them pretty hard. I'm sadly not able to accurately show you how to make every single possible armor piece, but I still want to offer you a helping hand. I'll give you a general idea of how things work so you will be able to adapt these techniques to countless different costumes in the future.

The following shoulder example might not be the most elaborate design but it will introduce you to a few new techniques and materials. Additionally you'll get a helpful basic pattern for your collection. I hope this tutorial will be the beginning of a gigantic pair of pauldrons for your upcoming costume.

Getting the Right Pattern Shape

Next to the bracer and the breastplate, let's add a shoulder armor pattern to our growing repertoire. Cosplay is just like any other hobby in that it will go a lot quicker if you've done it before. You can simply use already existing material to make new things a lot faster. Additionally it's just a matter of time until you have nice base patterns for pretty much every part of your body.

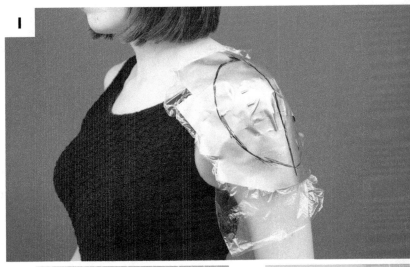

1 Wrap Your Shoulder and Mark the Shape

You already know the drill, right? Use plastic wrap and duct tape strips to cover your shoulder. Apply shorter strips to avoid wrinkles and bumps. As always, it will be hard wrapping yourself, so ask a friend for help. Draw a middle line and make a big circle around your shoulder. This will be the basic shape for this project.

2 Cut the Pattern

Take the plastic wrap off and cut out the marked pattern. You should get two leaf-shaped pieces.

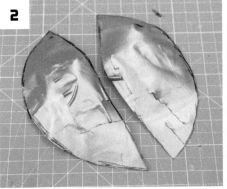

3 Trace the Pattern

Press the pattern pieces flat and choose the one with fewer wrinkles. You'll mirror the shape, so just one good shape is fine. Since your tape piece will be pretty baggy, it's best to trace it on paper.

4 Draw Your Design

Use this template to sketch a more advanced shoulder armor design. Keep in mind that this flat piece will be shaped round again, so try to take this into account when drawing your design.

HOW TO CREATE A PAULDRON
Craft Foam and Worbla

Why Worbla this time? It's easier to stretch the material into spherical shapes, which is perfect for a pauldron. On the next pages you'll notice that I also want to show you a new type of primer that works well with this thermoplastic.

1 Cover the Pieces in Worbla

Transfer your cutout paper pattern twice to craft foam and cover everything with Worbla—just like in the bracer example. Heat your parts up equally and press the middle seam together.

2 Shape the Piece

Just like with our last foam example, an acrylic sphere is really helpful for shaping Worbla. Apply some parting wax on the sphere to prevent your build from sticking to the surface. Then heat the Worbla and form it around the sphere.

3 Seal and Sand the Middle

Get rid of the middle gap by adding a thin strip of Worbla and sanding down the edge. The result should be a nice pauldron that fits perfectly over your shoulder. If not just reheat the material and give it another try. Even years of practice will not prevent you from having to redo things sometimes.

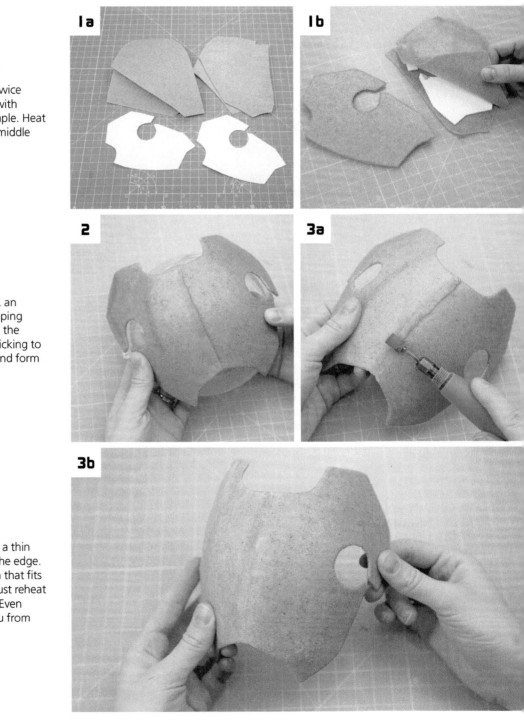

Working with Spray Filler

Worbla can be primed with many different products to get a clean and smooth surface. In my first example I used wood glue. While it works perfectly fine, the result might still have some bumps and imperfections. These little flaws disappear under acrylic paint and are usually not an issue. If you want to apply a spray paint, though, this might be a problem.

One way to achieve a perfectly clean base is by using spray filler. This product originated from the car industry to fix scratches. You should be able to find it easily in your local hardware store.

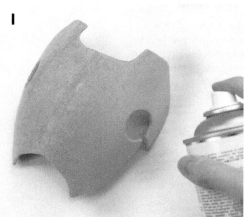

1 Start Spraying the Filler

For the right application it's best to spray outside or in a well-ventilated area. This stuff is toxic, so get your respiratory protection ready. Shake the can for about a minute and spray a thin coat from a distance of 8" (20cm) all over your build.

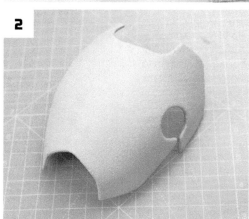

2 Spray the Whole Piece

Let it dry a bit and repeat spraying. It might take a few hours until a thickly applied layer is dry enough for the next step. You're going to have to sand most of the primer away again, so don't worry if your spray coat is too thick.

3 Sand the Primer

Once the primer has completely dried, it's time for some sanding work. A small orbital sander is really useful here, but you can achieve the same effect with patience and sandpaper. First use a low grit of 100 or 120 and switch to 180 or 240 to get a super smooth surface. What should we never forget when sanding something? Right, your respiratory and eye protection. It helps to sand over a powered on vacuum cleaner since it will suck away most of the dust you create.

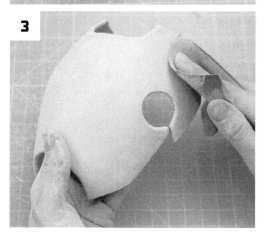

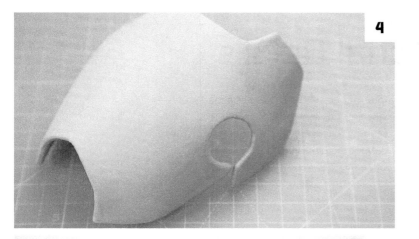

4 Finish Sanding

For this example I first used my orbital sander with 120 grit paper, sprayed on another coat and sanded it by hand afterwards with a grit of 180. The first layer helps fill up big gaps and get rid of bumps, while the second one makes the piece really nice and smooth. Don't worry if you end up sanding all the way through to your Worbla. If that happens, just apply more spray filler and sand it down again.

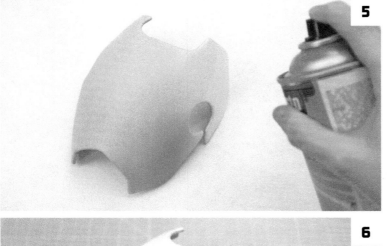

5 Start Adding Color

Instead of acrylics, this time I used a glossy white automotive spray paint. Shake the can thoroughly, spray a test spot and then apply a thin paint coat over your armor piece.

6 Cover the Whole Piece

Continue spraying and cover the whole shoulder piece. You may have to let the thin layers dry before applying the next one.

When working with a brush there will always be little brushstrokes no matter how clean you apply the color. It's impossible to get a perfectly even application of paint. A spray, however, will give you a great result in only a few seconds. This makes it very suitable for technical looking costume pieces.

Safety First!

Protective Gear: I used spray cans for both the primer as well as the paint job. The fumes from these products are not only flammable but also toxic when breathed in. To protect your health, always wear protection and work in well-ventilated areas.

Safe Work Spaces: I actually built a little homemade spray booth using a lockable IKEA closet, a big air pump and some filters. All you need is a box with a hole, a filter to catch the particles and something that sucks in the fumes and blows them out the window. Or simply go to your backyard.

HOW TO CREATE A PAULDRON
Sculpting Additional Details

A couple of parts are still missing, so the shoulder piece isn't completely done. A good way to create big sturdy Worbla pieces is to stuff them with thick EVA foam. Carve an element out and cover it with a protective coat of Worbla. Details that are made this way will be sturdy and lightweight.

Adding interesting details is just a matter of patience and the will to try things out. Set your creativity free; there is no right or wrong way to create something amazing as long as you reach your goal. Use every opportunity to experiment with new materials and techniques.

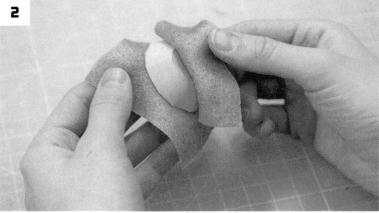

1 Cut the Shoulder Detail

For the round piece on top of my shoulder armor, I carved a little circle of foam with a hobby knife before smoothing the edge with the Dremel.

2 Cover the Foam with Worbla

I covered the foam piece with Worbla on both sides and heated up the material to activate the adhesive. Then I cut away excess material using tiny round nail scissors.

3 Attach the Shoulder Detail

I used my heat gun on the inner side of the shoulder pieces as well as the new detail shape to connect both using a little pressure.

You'll have to decide if you want to prime your extra pieces first and attach them later or attach them now and prime them later. It doesn't make much difference for this small example. Once you're working on a big elaborate costume part, you will have to plan ahead, though. It might be difficult to reach every gap and edge after you've put everything together.

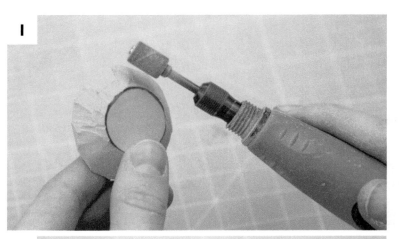

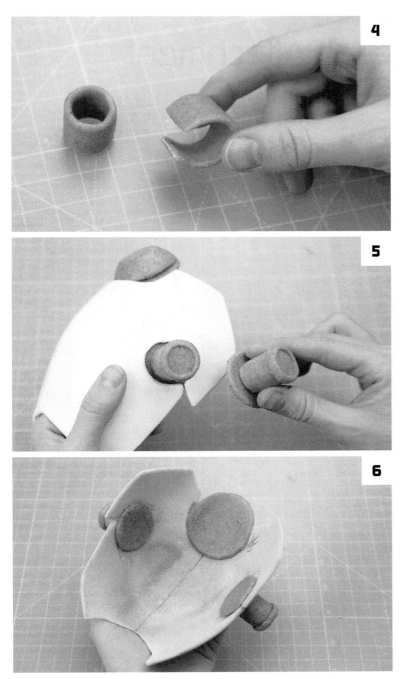

4 Create More Detail Pieces

I sculpted two more hollow cylinders by covering little craft foam strips with Worbla and connecting them at their ends.

5 Attach the Other Details

Next, I placed the elements on slightly larger circles, heated them up and attached them to the inner side of the pauldron.

6 Scratch Away Primer if Needed

The inner side of my build was covered with spray primer, which can make the attachment difficult. To make the additional pieces stick properly, I simply scratched the primer away.

Try Different Techniques

At this point you may wonder why I didn't just use spray filler for all the previous examples in this book. It's simply much easier to sand a blank round piece instead of getting into all the gaps and angles of a highly decorated bracer. This would have taken a lot more time and would have looked only marginally better. My techniques are here to inspire you. They're not the only way to create something. Just find the technique that you like the most.

Priming, Painting and Attachment

Follow the same process that you've done in previous demos. Prime the Worbla with white glue, then add color with acrylic paint. For the attachment of this piece, I chose to use magnets. Using magnets can make it easy for a piece to just snap into place on your costume.

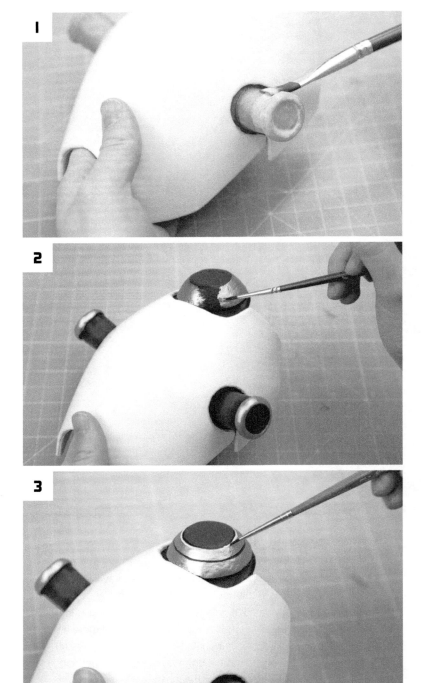

1 Prime the Detail Pieces

I used a few layers of simple white glue to prime the additional parts, but I had to be careful not to get too much on the already finished shiny white paint.

2 Add Color

I gave the additional parts a black basecoat with acrylic paint once the glue was dry. Then I took a highly pigmented silver color and brushed it onto the shapes to add dimension and interest. The white glossy spray paint already acts a lot like a varnish, and you can wipe away any black or silver color that you might have accidentally gotten onto it.

3 Paint Edging Details

I painted the final edging details on the shapes with black acrylic and a small brush. Then I sealed the newly added acrylic color parts by applying a final layer of brush-on satin varnish.

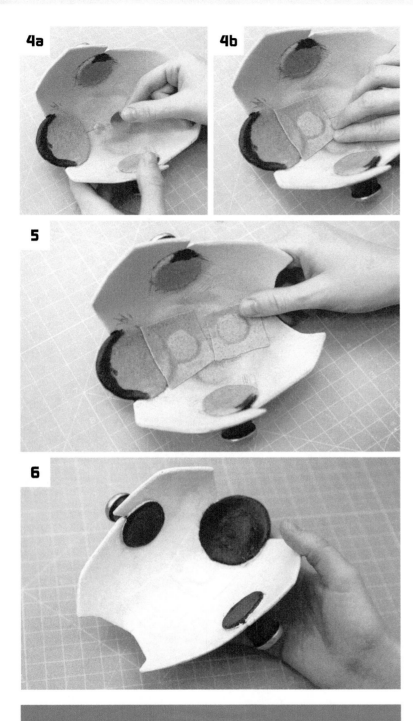

4 Attach a Magnet

The shoulder armor needed to be mounted directly to my cloth-covered arm, so why not just snap it on, right? I got a few rare earth magnets on eBay. These 10mm magnets are much stronger than regular ones and are perfect for costume attachments of all kinds. However, while it is hard to pull two of them apart, it's quite easy to break their connection by sliding them down. There will always be people who bump into you at a convention, so the chance of your shoulder piece being ripped off is pretty high. Better be safe and use at least two of them.

To attach the magnets, I simply mounted them on a drop of hot glue, heated up the inner side of the shoulder and added an additional layer of Worbla on top to seal it.

5 Attach Another Magnet

I repeated step 5 and attached the second magnet a little bit beneath the first one to better secure my pauldron attachment.

6 Paint the Inside

Once the Worbla cooled down, I painted the inside with lacquer so I got a nice finished piece. Painting the shoulder from the inside might seem like a waste of time, but you never know if looking at your costume from a different angle will reveal unfinished pieces. If you're really passionate, you will find yourself spending hours upon hours working on things nobody but you will notice.

Get a Variety of Magnets

Since you're already buying nice magnets, why not expand your shopping list a tiny bit? They are available in all kinds of shapes and sizes, and it's good to have different ones at home. You can get them really cheap online. Magnets are handy for all kinds of projects and costume pieces, and you never know when you may need one.

Prop tip: Did you know that contact glue has a stronger connection than most magnets? This works especially well with foam. You can often just glue your magnets directly to your foam armor as a ready-to-go attachment. Why not try it out for your next project?

7 Add Magnets to the Fabric

I applied magnet counterparts to the fabric part of the costume. I simply glued them on and covered them afterward with an additional piece of fabric. This way they stay in place better. If you're just buying a body suit for your armor costume, this technique totally works, and you still don't have to work with a sewing machine!

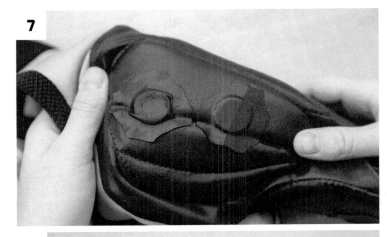

8 Consider Optional Extra Security

A more advanced approach would be to sew the magnets inside your suit. In any case just make sure to have them facing the right way or they won't work. If you want to be extra safe, you can also add an additional tiny D-ring to the top. Just build a little counterpart on your armor piece and you're prepared for pretty much everything.

Well, that's it! Now jump into your magnetic costume, attach your armor pieces with a loud snap and inspire other artists with your attractive attachment solution.

Overwatch Symmetra

The character Symmetra from Blizzard's game *Overwatch* was a pretty diverse mixed-media project. With her sleek robotic arm and the visor helmet, I had to figure out a new technique to create really smooth armor. Additionally, I had to improve my sewing skills to make the dress and was also challenged by her glowing sci-fi blaster, the Photon Projector. After reading the previous pages you surely know that I made a pattern for her mechanical arm and shaped the pieces out of Worbla. I covered everything in spray primer, sanded it down and finished it off with a glossy white spray paint. The same worked for the helmet as well. To shape the gun, I simply printed out a screenshot, cut it into sections and traced this template onto a few layers of thick EVA foam. After sanding the individual parts, I covered them with Worbla and attached them to each other. Finally, I put a few soldered LEDs inside to give it a fancy light effect. Painting the gun actually works the same as painting the pauldron.

Photo by eosAndy: eosandy.com

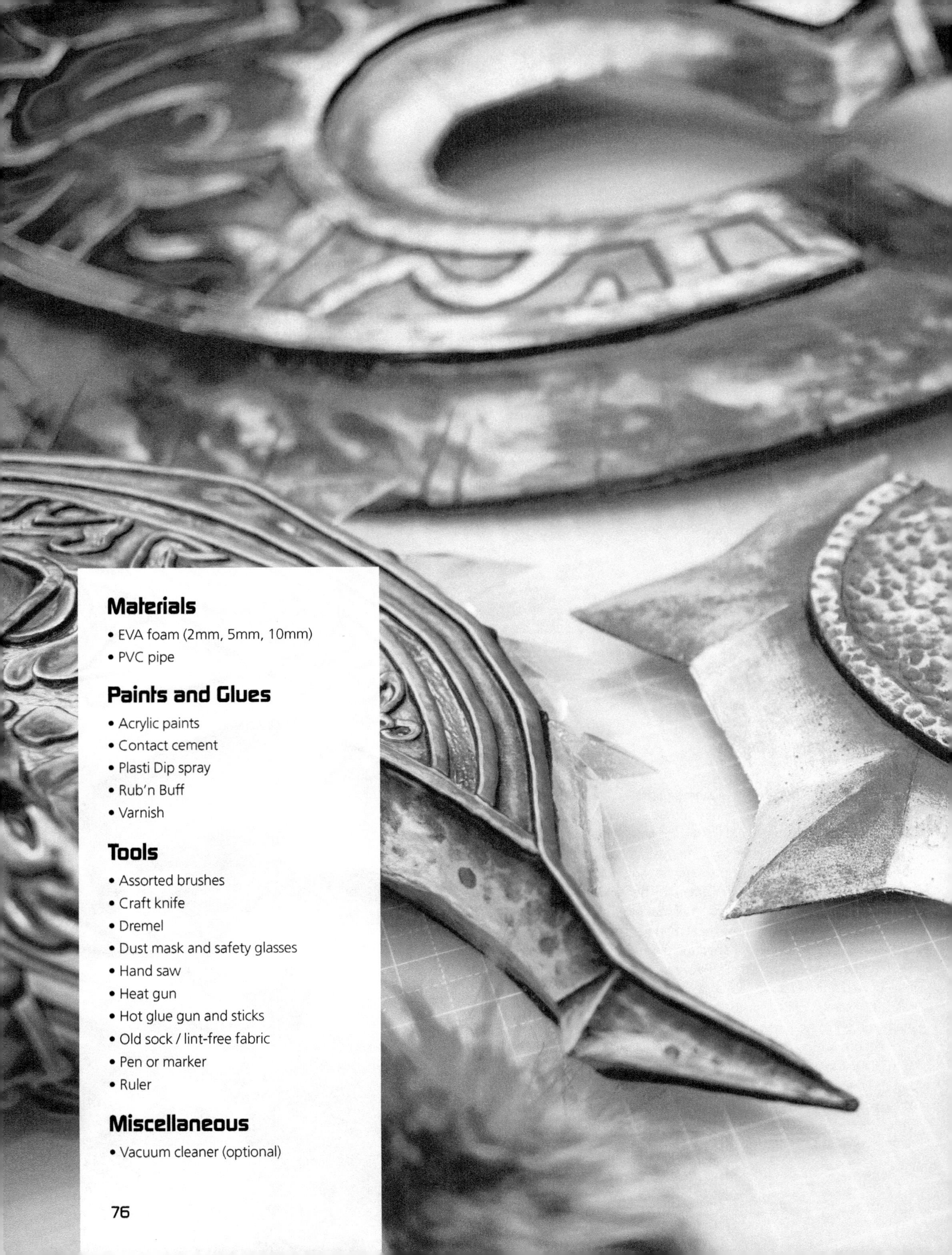

Materials

- EVA foam (2mm, 5mm, 10mm)
- PVC pipe

Paints and Glues

- Acrylic paints
- Contact cement
- Plasti Dip spray
- Rub'n Buff
- Varnish

Tools

- Assorted brushes
- Craft knife
- Dremel
- Dust mask and safety glasses
- Hand saw
- Heat gun
- Hot glue gun and sticks
- Old sock / lint-free fabric
- Pen or marker
- Ruler

Miscellaneous

- Vacuum cleaner (optional)

How to Create an Axe

When building awesome props and costumes, the possibilities are endless. Some materials are expensive, some tools are way out of reach for ordinary mortals and some projects require a whole warehouse of space. The following axe example, however, will be cheap, easy to put together and needs only a small table with minimal tools. Why an axe? Well, because axes are awesome and make you feel like a Viking just by holding them!

First you need a blueprint. You can either draw a shape on some paper or your computer, print out a screenshot or simply start crafting by following your own imagination. For this example I created a clean line drawing and printed it out life size over multiple pages. This print will be our reference throughout the next few pages.

Shaping EVA Foam

The material I chose this time is the same high-density EVA foam that I used for my breastplate but double the thickness, so 10mm. It's lightweight, cheap and really easy to work with; perfect for creating props.

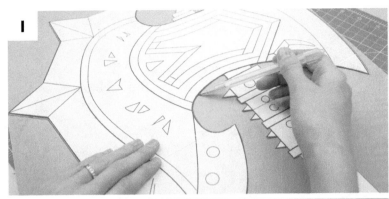

1 Trace Your Pattern

To start your project, grab a pen and trace the outline of the printed blade pattern onto the foam. To get more volume for the axe, repeat this step for another foam piece.

2 Cut the Foam

All you need to cut EVA foam is a sharpened hobby knife. Place the blade on the foam in a straight 90-degree angle and follow the lines you marked. If you're not getting through the material in one swipe, make sure that your blade is sharp and go again. Curves and tight angles in particular are hard to reach sometimes, but you'll get better with practice. Keep in mind that you can clean up messy cuts with your Dremel, so don't worry if your first try isn't perfect.

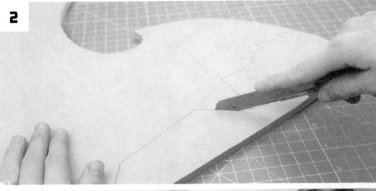

3 Add Contact Cement

After cutting out both shapes, apply a thin layer of contact cement to both pieces.

4 Adhere the Pieces

Line up the pieces and press them together. It's not easy to precisely place the pieces, but as long as the glue hasn't dried out completely, it's still possible to adjust their position a tiny bit. This gets harder the bigger your pieces are, but you can always cut away more material later to align your edges.

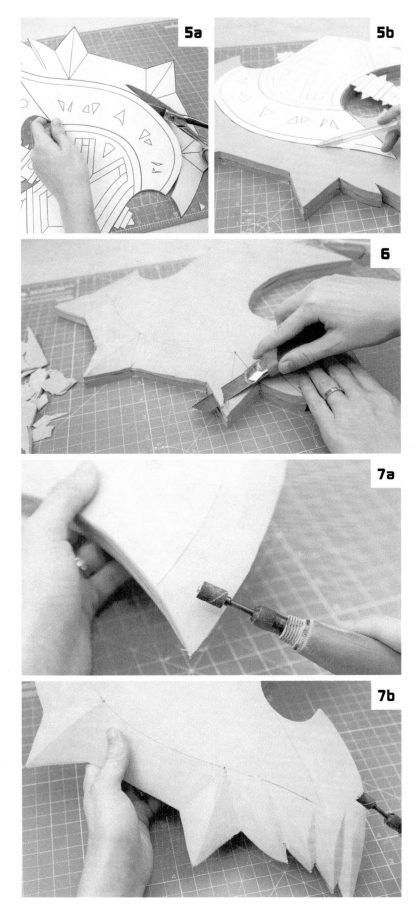

5 Mark Where You'll Trim Away

Besides serving as a basic outline of your prop, a blueprint or drawing is also great to mark the areas you need to sand away. Mark on the sharp, angled blade of the axe and cut out the inner part of the pattern. Transfer the template onto the foam. This is helpful not only to get a nice blade later but to give you an idea of where you need to sand more or less away.

6 Trim the Foam

As you can see, I even used a ruler to mark the geometrical shapes of the blade. Sanding foam with a rotary tool will create a lot of dust and take a long time. If you want to avoid turning your room into a messy crafting cave, precut the material with a sharp knife. Work only on the surface and don't set your blade too deep. It's better to cut in many thin slices instead of removing too much material at once. You can always get rid of more but can't glue things back on. It's best to practice this on a separate scrap of foam first.

7 Clean the Carved Foam

Clean up your carving work with a Dremel. A simple sanding drum with a rough grit is sufficient. Go carefully over the rough and ridged edges of your foam and watch how it slowly becomes clean and smooth. If you've never worked with a Dremel before, start with something easy like the smooth, simple axe blade. Work in different directions and find a sanding technique you're comfortable with. You won't become a Dremel master overnight, so set your tool on low speed first and get faster once you're ready. Always wear eye and respiratory protection.

If you have a vacuum cleaner, turn it on and work over the hose to gather most of the flying dust where it is created. This will be quite noisy, but you'll keep your air clean and won't have to worry too much about cleaning up later.

Attaching a Handle

At this point you should have a pretty blade, but you still need a grip. A great material for that job is PVC pipe from the hardware store. Try to get one with a good diameter that fits nicely into your hand.

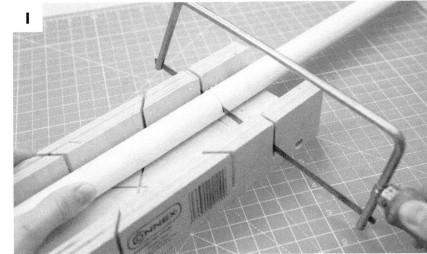

1 Cut a PVC Handle

Mark the PVC pipe for the right handle length or use a template rig to help with the length. Cut it to the right length using a hand saw or your Dremel saw tip.

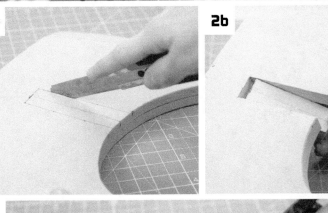

2 Mark and Cut the Handle Placement

Let's bring both parts together. Measure the width of your rod and mark where you want to place it. Set your grip straight into the foam. Your pipe doesn't need to get all the way through the axe, but it's better to slide it in as deep as possible. Cut out the marked area with your hobby knife.

3 Adhere the Pipe Grip

Attaching the grip is no witchcraft, either. Just lay in the pipe and cover it on both sides with hot glue. If you placed your cuts right, it should fit perfectly into the foam gap. Don't spare the glue; make the connection really strong. You don't want the tip of your axe to come flying off as soon as you swing it, right?

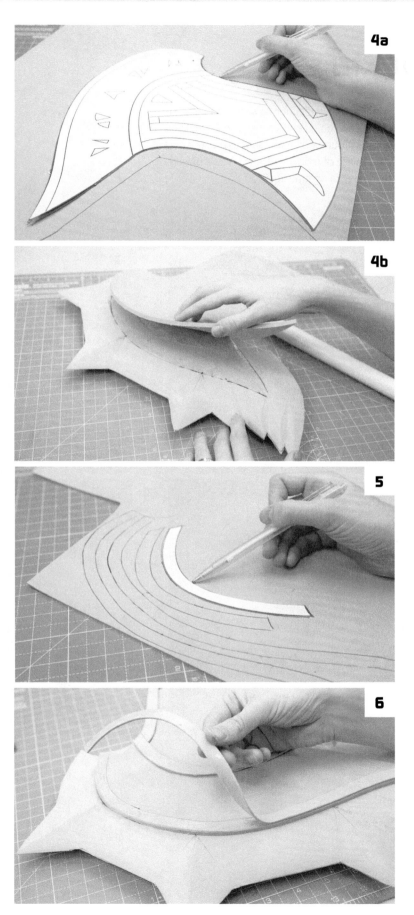

4a

4b

5

6

4 Cut and Adhere a Thin Top Layer

Next come the details. I used the original template to cut out a covering piece from 5mm foam. I added contact cement to the axe as well as to the additional element and pressed both parts together. For details, thinner sheets of foam work better, otherwise your prop will look too bulky and thick.

5 Trace and Cut Design Elements

The same principle applies to smaller elements as well. I cut out the lines from the paper blueprint and transfered their shape to the thinner 2mm EVA foam. They were then cut out as well.

6 Adhere the Elements to the Axe

The strips were glued onto the axe with contact cement. I used a few simple lines, but they were enough to make the axe look more interesting.

Realistic Foam Textures

To make your flat foam look like real metal or wood, just add cool textures with a Dremel. Axe handles are usually made from tree branches, so you have to sand deep lines into your foam. The hammered texture of the blade itself is created by covering it with countless little craters using a round sanding tip. If you're worried that you will ruin your work, make sure to practice on a scrap piece of foam in advance. You'll master this technique in no time at all.

1 Measure the Handle

Measure the handle's circumference and length. Add a few millimeters to the width measurement, though, since you want to bend the foam around the plastic.

2 Cut Foam and Wrap the Handle

Transfer the handle measurement numbers to 2mm EVA foam. You should end up with a rectangular piece that fits perfectly around your PVC rod. Add contact cement to both the foam and the handle and press them together very carefully.

3 Dremel Lines into the Handle

This new foam skin is perfect for adding texture through sanding and carving. All you need is your trusty Dremel, a few different sanding tips and a little bit of practice. To make the handle look like real wood, use the standard sanding drum. By using only the very edge of the drum, you're able to carve deep lines like those on tree bark.

4 Turn Foam into Wood

Keep doing this all over the grip from top to bottom. Add a few circles here and there—like the knotholes on trees—and draw most lines parallel to each other to get a consistent and convincing texture. In only a few minutes your foam handle has been transformed into a perfect replica of a real wooden handle.

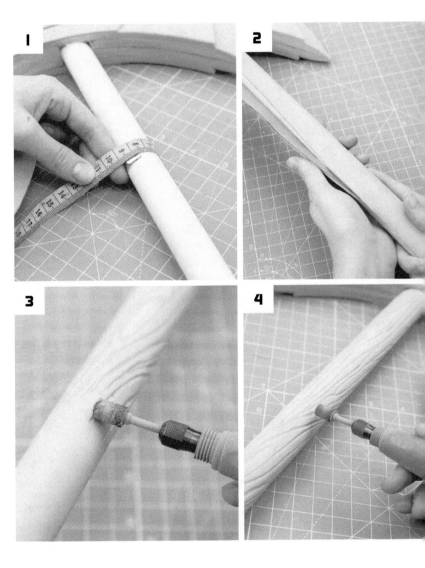

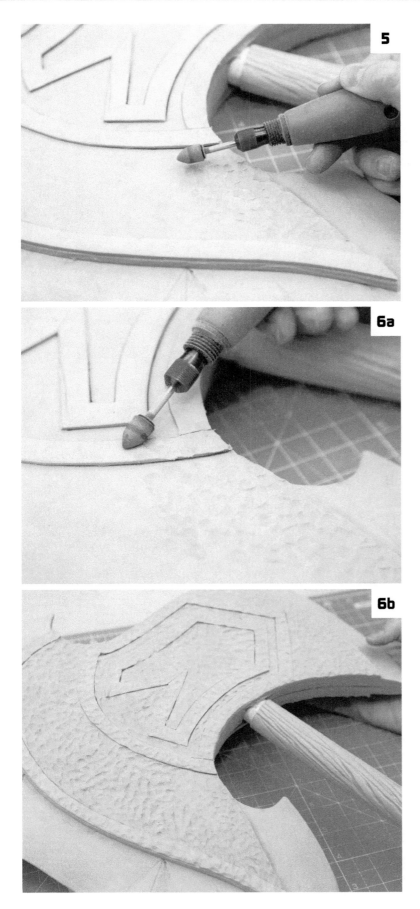

5 Sand Little Craters into the Blade

Besides wood, axes are supposed to be made of metal. So the next texture I'll show you is the look of hammered steel. If you do a Google image search for that phrase, you'll notice it usually looks like a bunch of circles squished together. Use a sanding tip with a round end and press it lightly against the foam. That way you're getting rid of a little bit of material and can control where you place the holes next to each other.

6 Turn Foam into Metal

Repeat this all over the additional details you glued to the blade of the axe. Avoid creating a uniform texture since it might end up too regular and artificial. Place your little craters randomly and in slightly different angles. It should look as if a sweaty blacksmith hammered over this axe with a giant, hard-to-control hammer. This wouldn't turn out sleek and perfect.

7 Add Grip Details

Now that the axe blade itself is done, apply a few additional details to the grip. A simple wooden rod could be enough, but in this case I thought it would be boring. So let's add more metal pieces. Measure the circumference around the foam handle, cut out a piece of foam to fit and glue it on. Don't place foam details over every part of your prop though. A few here and there are okay. You still want to be able to hold the axe after all.

8 Close the Bottom Grip

To round off the end of the handle and hide the end of the pipe, cut out a circular piece of foam and glue it on with contact cement.

9 Add Texture

Add texture to the new details you've added. Repeat the same metallic texture technique with the Dremel that you used on the main blade.

10 Clean up the Foam

Unfortunately, all the sanding made the surface of the foam very rough, messy and dusty. Directly painting it in this state will be difficult. Luckily, it's really easy to clean the surface. Grab the heat gun and carefully melt away the foam leftovers on the axe. The heat gets rid of tiny dust particles and larger crumbs. Take your time. Your final result should look slightly shiny, clean and free of dust.

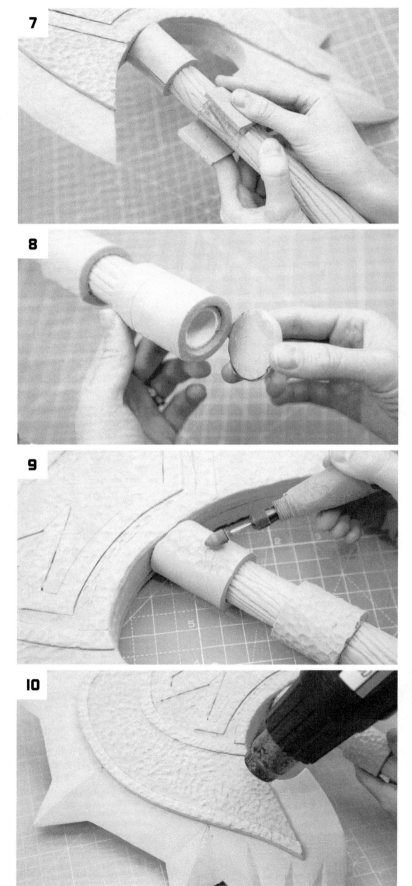

Sealing EVA Foam

Another important step before the actual paint job is priming the surface. Even your heat-sealed foam is still prone to cracks and wrinkles if you bend or stretch it too much. I've already covered a few techniques in this book, but I still want to keep it interesting. So instead of brushing on some Plasti Dip, I'm going to spray it on this time. This will create a clean and protective rubber coating in just a few moments. It's perfect for EVA foam, but you will have to work in a fitting environment since the dust is toxic and very hard to get off again. For the sake of getting better photos I simply put it on my table, but you should definitely go outside or use a spray booth for this step. Don't forget to wear eye and respiratory protection.

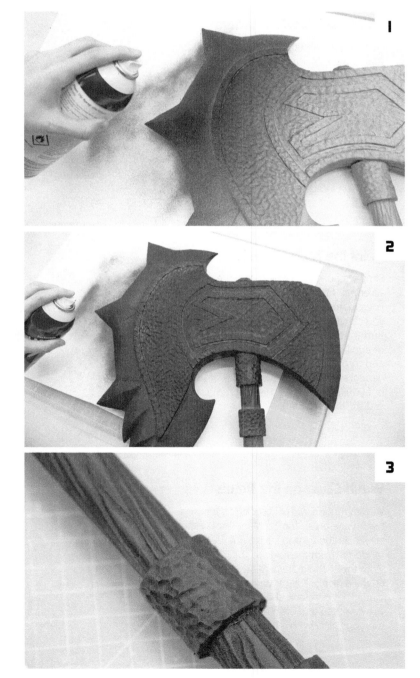

1 Start Spraying Plasti Dip

Heat up your Plasti Dip can in a pot of hot water, then take it out and shake it for about a minute. Otherwise it may spray huge and messy drops. Apply a good covering coat all over your foam from a distance of around 8" (20cm). Your axe should be covered in a shiny wet application, but avoid creating any thick drops.

2 Add More Layers of Primer

Wait a bit for the first layer to dry and then add a few more layers of primer until you're satisfied with the thickness. Usually you need somewhere between three and five coats.

3 Clean up the Primer

If you got black Plasti Dip like me, you can directly start with the paint job. Otherwise just cover your work in a basic coat of the right color.

Painting and Weathering

Turning boring foam into a realistic-looking metal axe isn't wizardry. All you need is a piece of fabric, acrylic paint and a little bit of patience. No artistic skills are necessary at all. As always, try to find quality products with a high amount of pigmentation. There are countless shiny special effect colors available, so keep your eyes open for them. They are surely useful for many other projects as well.

1 Paint the Wooden Handle

Applying a realistic paint job isn't hard. Just grab a piece of lint-free fabric or some old socks. Stick your finger inside the fabric, dip it into a bit of brown acrylic paint and start smearing the paint over your sealed foam handle. Start with a darker brown paint and go on to a brighter version afterwards. By spreading the paint only on the surface, the carved lines stay black while everything else turns into a natural brown. As you can see, the result looks like real wood!

2 Paint the Metal Details

Simply repeat this same technique with silver paint for the metallic textures that you created before. Instead of acrylic paint you can also use a product called Rub'n Buff that was created especially for this way of application. Smear only on the surface and try to keep the tiny craters black or dark gray. It might be a bit messy at first, but you'll be able to achieve an amazingly realistic look of metal.

3 Brush Silver on the Blade

While working with old socks is super fun, use a wide brush for the blade. Apply some acrylic on the tip and stroke quickly and randomly from the edge to the inner side. With this technique you'll automatically create a nice gradient, which will make your blade look crisp and sharp. If you want to, you can then add even more highlights if you mix your silver with a bit of white.

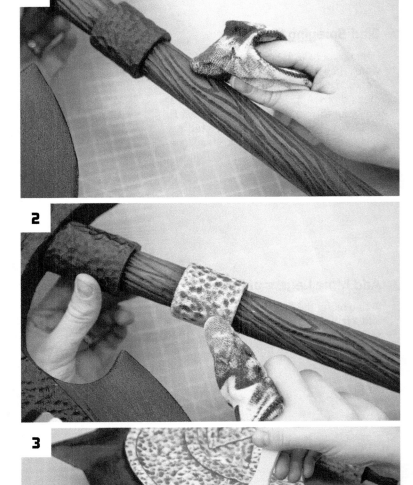

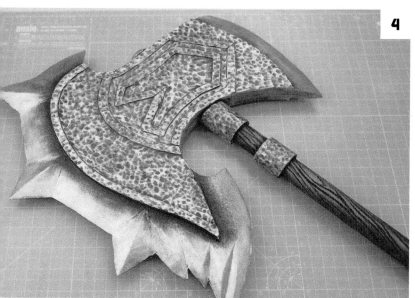

4 Finish the Metal Blade

Finish working the silver around the blade edges. While this already looks very cool, the axe still seems like it came right out of the forge. Everything is a bit too clean and new. To give this prop some age, it's time to add some weathering effects.

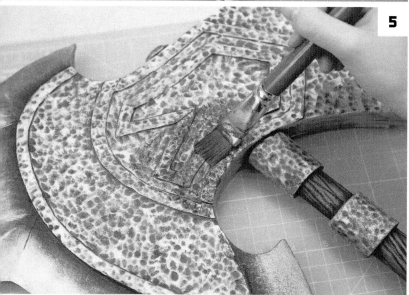

5 Start Weathering

This step is really fun, but it should only be applied to armor pieces or weapons where it makes sense and helps tell a story. A mighty Viking who came back from his yearly raiding tour will look like he has seen some action, while a beautiful wizard who fights only from a distance will still look shiny and new even after a long battle.

For weathering you can go out hiking with your axe and pull it through puddles, rain and dirt or just fake all that with acrylics. Mix a dark brown with a lot of water and spread it all over your previous paint job. Yes, this feels like destroying all the hard work you put in before, but believe me when I say it's worth it. Your paint should still be pretty wet, even after a couple of minutes.

6 Wipe Away the Excess and Keep Weathering

Grab a tissue and wipe the paint away. Some acrylic will remain in the corners and crevices of your prop and that's exactly what you want. In real life the mighty blade would fall into mud and dirt and be cleaned afterwards as well. It's basically the same thing. Just repeat this step until you're happy with the result. It's critical to alter your paint job just right so that it looks straight out of an epic fantasy saga.

7 Add Rust Effects

Metal, especially iron, does another thing when it's exposed to moisture like rain and dirt—it rusts. There are multiple ways to achieve a convincing rust effect. Some involve applying chemicals and acids to make real metal powder rust on your surface painting. We'll keep it simple though and use acrylics.

Mix brown and orange until you have a rusty color. Instead of using a lot of water and acrylics, just use the paint at a few deliberately chosen spots. The key is to find a few areas of your prop where water might have collected over time. This works especially well for raised edges and details. Place some rust there and immediately wipe most of it away. The leftovers in the edges and corners are what you want for this effect.

8 Darken the Shadows on the Blade

Creating a realistic-looking replica doesn't mean only good craftsmanship, but also a good feeling for the story of your prop. An old battle axe might be dirty as well as rusty, so add some splatter to your prop with a watery, paint-soaked brush. Also darken the spikes of the blade to get additional contrast.

9 Seal the Paint

Feel free to seal your finished paint job with a bit of varnish afterwards. Sometimes giving a prop a nice paint job means making everything look pretty first and then going all out to destroy it again. It's really fun! You want to protect that messy paint job too though. That final varnish is important.

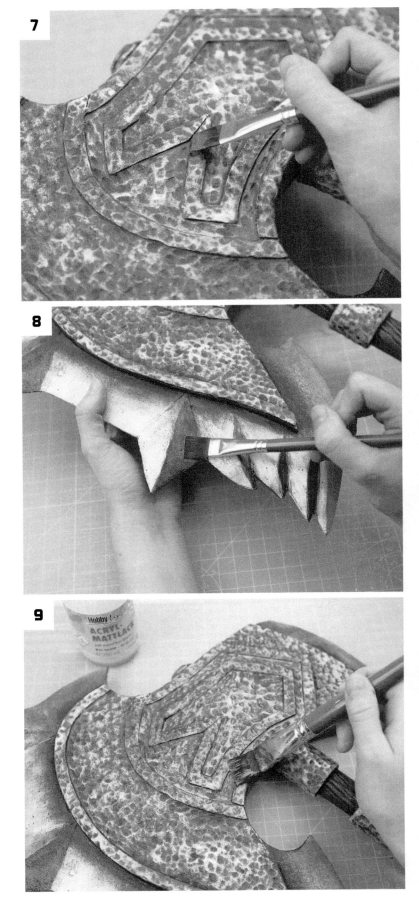

Diablo III Barbarian

The Barbarian from the video game *Diablo III* was actually one of my very first armor projects. It was also the first time I worked with Worbla. I had to experiment a lot until I found techniques that I was happy with. Trying new things out, however, is what makes a project exciting. My Barbarian helped me a lot to learn more about armor making, while also teaching me new attachment methods and how to weather a costume properly. Additionally, I love to jump into the shoes of powerful female characters. She is wild and dangerous but still beautiful. Wearing this costume gives me a lot of confidence, and it's just fun to swing my axe around at a convention. To this day this costume is still one of my favorites and will always have a special place in my heart.

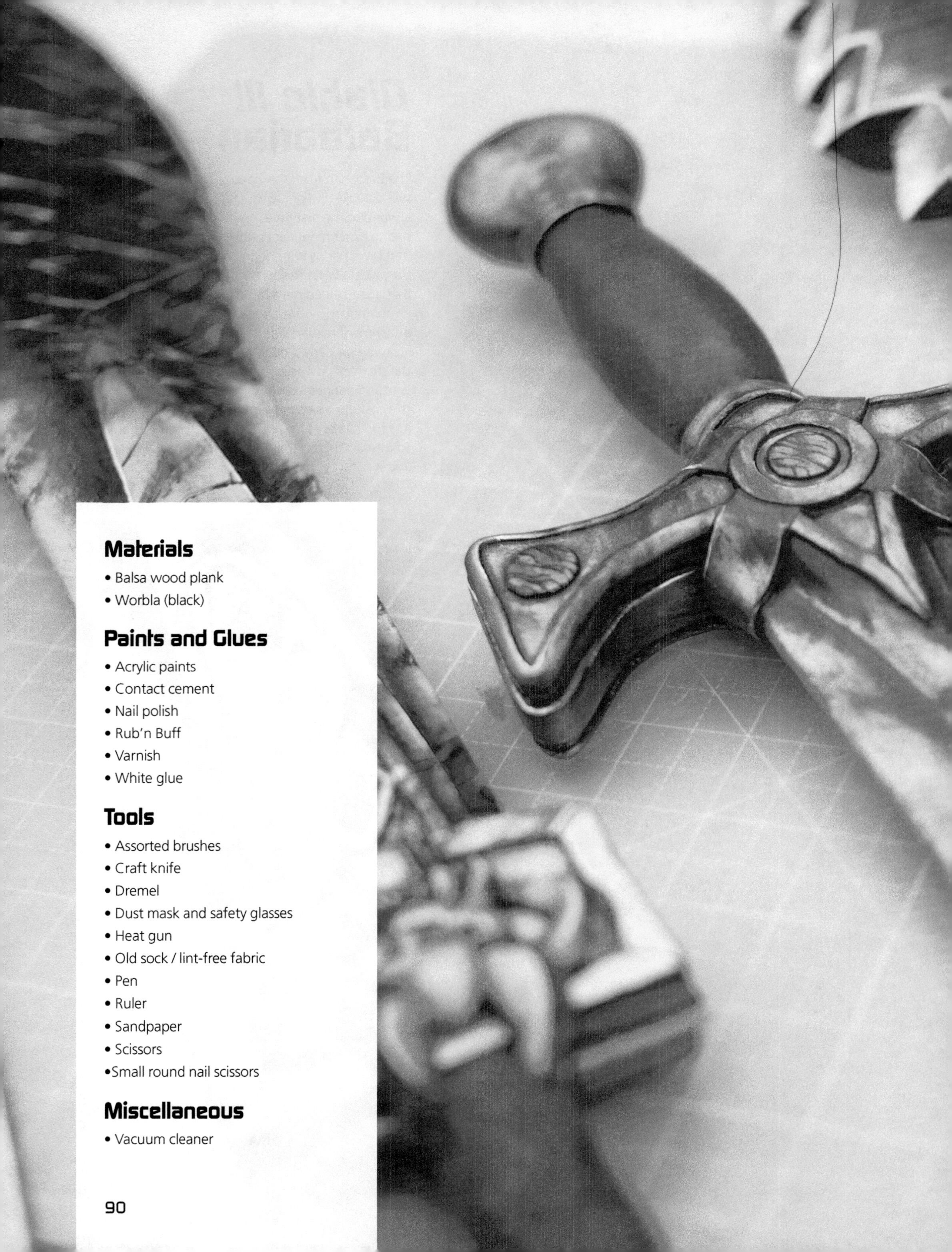

Materials

- Balsa wood plank
- Worbla (black)

Paints and Glues

- Acrylic paints
- Contact cement
- Nail polish
- Rub'n Buff
- Varnish
- White glue

Tools

- Assorted brushes
- Craft knife
- Dremel
- Dust mask and safety glasses
- Heat gun
- Old sock / lint-free fabric
- Pen
- Ruler
- Sandpaper
- Scissors
- Small round nail scissors

Miscellaneous

- Vacuum cleaner

How to Create a Sword

For the last example in my book, I want to show you how to get a solid Worbla sword with a wooden core. Swords are essential for many costumes and can be a great weekend project for Halloween as well. It's totally fine to buy a cheap plastic toy in a store, but I promise you it's a lot more fun to actually make one yourself.

If you search for online tutorials, you will find countless ways to create a cool blade. From cardboard to real steel, you'll find every possible material choice. My solution is something in between and will give you a lightweight but durable prop.

Cutting and Shaping Balsa Wood

Just like with the axe, you first need to get some blueprints. For this example I chose Xena's sword from the cult classic 1990s TV show. I searched for a few reference pictures online and then drew an outline myself. You can do this on your computer, by hand or even simply print out a good photo or screenshot. It's a bit easier to work with clean lines, so I went the printing route. After printing out your chosen reference, simply cut it out.

1 Trace the Pattern

With the finished blueprint in your hands it's time to transfer the shape to your material of choice. For this example I am using balsa wood, which you can buy in planks of different thicknesses. It's lightweight, cheap and can be cut using a regular hobby knife. It's basically like a mixture between wood and Styrofoam and is perfect for making cool swords of all kinds.

2 Cut the Wood

To get the shape of your sword, grab your hobby knife and cut along the traced pattern. Pull the knife all the way through the material and keep your blade straight. While cutting along the wood's grain works nicely, you'll need to be more forceful when working against it. Despite that, be extra careful with it—the material can break easily. This step is actually much easier if you get rid of smaller wood pieces first instead of trying to make one long cut at once.

3 Trace and Cut the Crossguard

As you can see, I split up my pattern into three layers of balsa wood: a single big one for the blade and two additional smaller ones to build up the handle. My balsa wood also wasn't wide enough for the whole sword, so I had to cut out some additional parts for the crossguard.

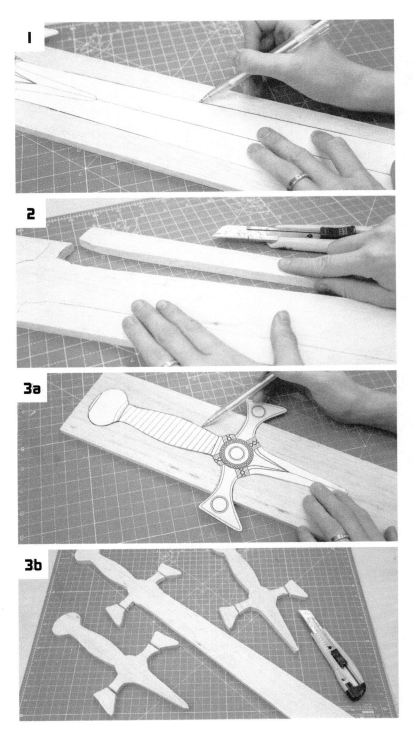

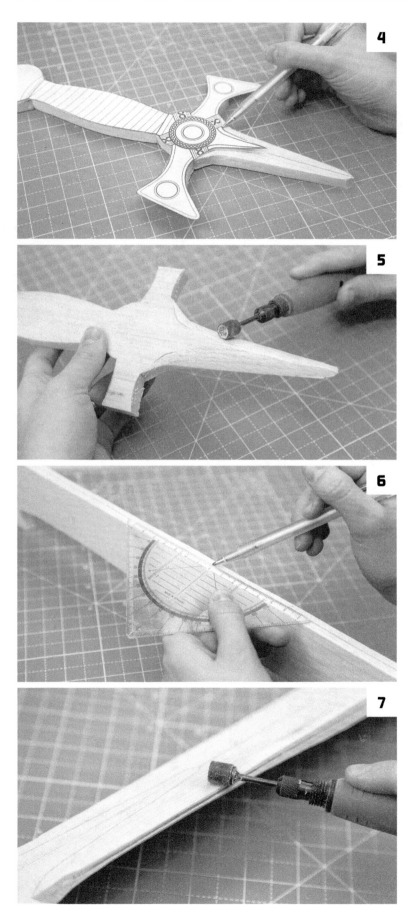

4 Mark Sanding Lines

A good blueprint is not only useful for getting the basic shapes, but also for marking where you need to sand or carve material away. Just cut your pattern into smaller and smaller elements until you have everything you need. Here I marked the area of the crossguard that I wanted to turn into a nice beveled edge.

5 Sand the Edges

Sand the side areas where you marked the edge lines. This works with a Dremel just as well as with a medium grit sandpaper.

6 Mark the Center of the Sword

To give the blade a symmetrical shape you will have to mark a few additional lines. Grab a ruler and draw a middle line along the edge and in the center of the sword's blade.

7 Sand the Edges to Angle the Sides

Use your Dremel to start sanding away material until you reach your markings. Just like with EVA foam, you can use a knife to get rid of some wood in advance. The sword blade needs to be thin and sharp on the edges but raised in the middle, so try to shape it accordingly. This step might be a little tricky, so take your time and check your work constantly. It's best to use sandpaper and long deliberate strokes for the finish. Be careful. Material that is gone stays gone forever.

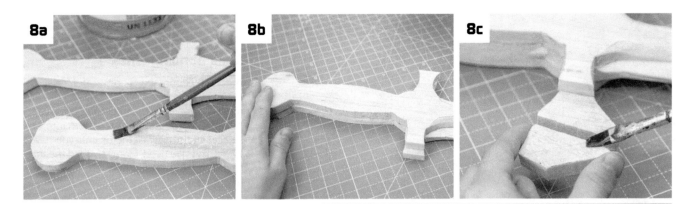

8a **8b** **8c**

8 Attach the Pieces

Let's put the puzzle together. While hot glue would be fine, contact cement works better. Apply contact cement on both sides, let it dry a few seconds and press both parts together. Connect the handle first and add the crossguard pieces afterward.

It's nearly impossible to cut and glue everything matching perfectly and without any visible gaps. Bumps and rough edges are normal. Use your Dremel and sand them down until it seems nice and clean again.

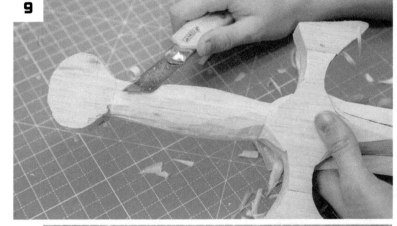

9

9 Carve the Handle

For the handle, you will need to do some carving work. Balsa wood is a very soft material, so all you need is a sharp knife. Cut away the edge corners first and then work your way toward a nearly smooth rounded piece. Only chip away the surface and don't cut too deep. Do this all around the grip.

10

10 Sand the Wood

Smooth your work afterwards with a piece of fine grit sandpaper. Sand around the handle and round out the edges.

11 Add Edge Details

Add a couple of beveled edges around the crossguard to get a softer, more natural look for your sword.

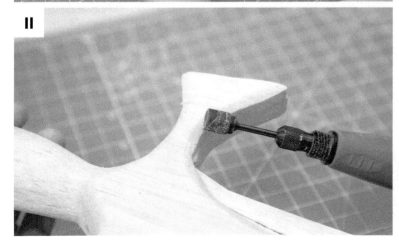

11

A Protective Worbla Coat

As you've probably noticed, it's really fun to craft with balsa wood. Balsa is, however, very breakable. It would be a shame if one mighty swing of your weapon broke it in two. To prevent that, you will need to give your wood work a protective coat on top. I already introduced you to regular brown Worbla, so now I want to tell you about black Worbla. This darker version of the thermoplastic has a much smoother surface and is perfect for a shiny metal look.

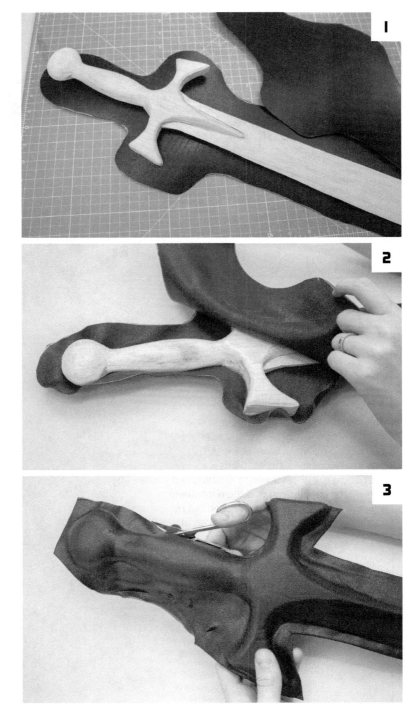

I Cut Two Large Pieces of Worbla

The technique is the same as in previous demos. Cut out two pieces of material slightly bigger than your blade and heat them up. You need to cover the core with the material completely, so make sure to cut out enough.

2 Heat the Worbla and Form It Around the Wood

After the material has reached the right temperature, carefully lay both sides onto your balsa wood and use your finger or a metal tool to press it into every nook and cranny of your sword. You want the Worbla to fit tightly around the wood like a second skin. Partially heat up your thermoplastic here and there to keep refining your work. The material will cool down fast and prevent you from working with it.

3 Trim Away the Excess

While your Worbla is still lukewarm, it's time to cut away the excess material. Trimming around the blade is easy, but reaching tight curves and angles with large scissors is tricky. I usually use tiny rounded nail scissors and trim away as much material as I can without damaging the Worbla coat.

Detail Work and Painting

Adding details will bring your sword to life. You can use tiny pieces of the original blueprint to cut out shapes in the right size and add double-layer black Worbla strips of different thicknesses to the grip. You can also combine regular brown thermoplastic with its black counterpart if you want a rougher looking surface for the crossguard.

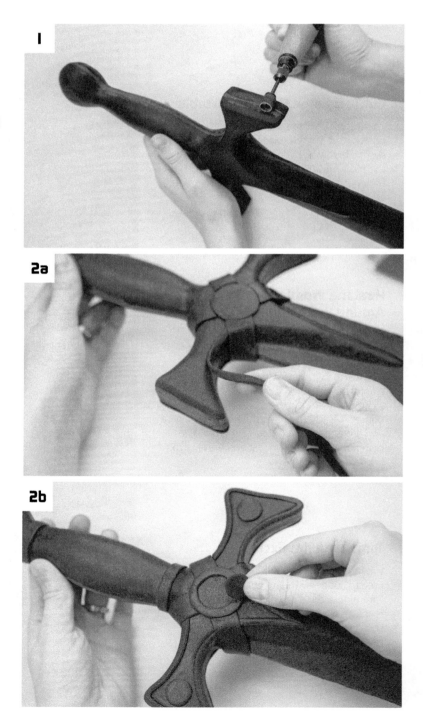

1 Sand the Seams

Use your Dremel and sand along the trimmed seams to get a nice, pretty blade. It will become dusty, so don't forget your safety gear and use a vacuum cleaner.

2 Cut and Add Details

The resulting Worbla sword is super durable and still lightweight. It's a perfect combination! Only a few missing details are left. Add stripes, circles, swirls and everything else that you want. Go nuts and use whatever helps you find the right shape for your final sword. Just don't overdo it by cramming in as much detail as you can fit.

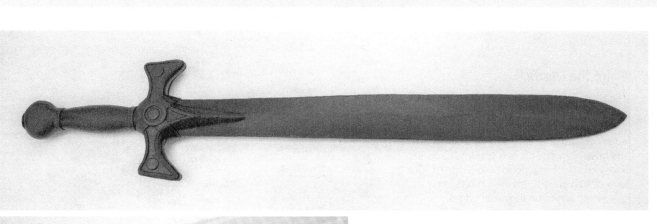

3 Prime the Sword

Black Worbla is a lot smoother than its brown sand-like brother. You will still need to use a primer, but this time only two or three layers of white glue will be enough. The result will be a sturdy and smooth surface, and your blade will be ready for a shiny, metallic paint job. Mix your white glue with a bit of water and apply thin layers to avoid getting any distracting drops on your blade.

4 Even out the Base Color

Since white glue does not always cure completely translucent and will leave a few white edges or spots, you can use black acrylic to give your sword an even base color. Black Worbla is—like the name implies—black, and if you're already happy with how the untreated surface looks, you can start directly dabbing on it.

5 Start Rubbing on Color

Instead of using brushes, I painted with old socks again. It's a fun technique for a realistic-looking result and will turn an old throwaway piece of cloth into an epic painting tool. With black as a basecoat, I went from dark to bright. The grip was supposed to be old bronze metal, so I used a fitting color variant of Rub'n Buff. Pull the fabric over your finger and dip it carefully into a little bit of the paint. This type of wax paint is highly pigmented, so even a tiny bit will cover a large area. I spread it over the crossguard and made sure to leave black space in between the detail shapes to get natural-looking shading.

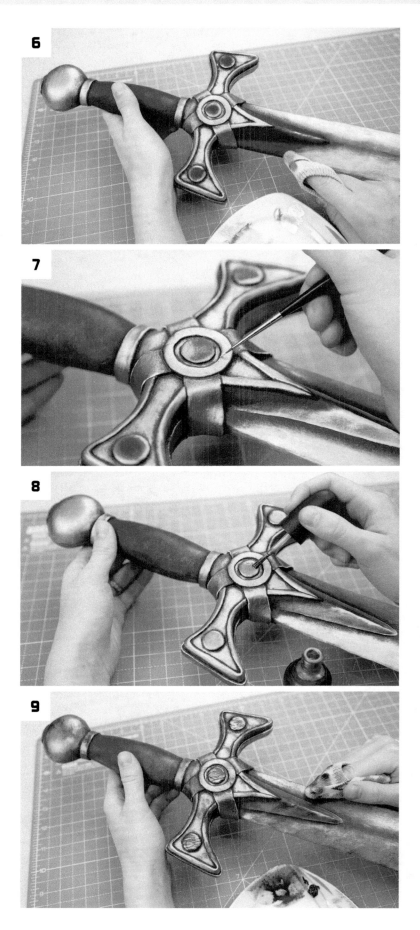

6 Paint the Blade

The blade got the same painting treatment, but I used silver Rub'n Buff this time. To get a nice gradient on this part, dab from the edges inward and leave a bit of shadow at the raised center. This way you'll get a darker line, which will help define the shape of your sword. To highlight this even more, you can add white acrylic on the outer edges.

7 Add Fine Lines and Highlights

You should have a nice, natural paint job. Leave it like that or add small white and black lines like I've shown you in my previous examples to better define the edges and add small highlights.

8 Add Pops of Color

The *Xena Warrior Princess* TV show was filmed in New Zealand, and her sword had three turquoise-colored New Zealand seashells on each side of the crossguard. I faked the look by using a few coats of shimmering nail polish and thin dark lines.

9 Add Weathering Effects

Now Xena's sword had to look used. I weathered the blade and crossguard by applying watered-down color and wiped it away afterward. Instead of using only black acrylic, I mixed in a few brown and green colors to make the effect more natural and dirtier. Also, think about where your character is from. If he or she lives in the desert, use bright sand-like colors or even add real sand for weathering. Try putting yourself in the shoes of your character and think about what types of places they could have been and what adventures they have lived through. Seal your work with matte varnish, and you have a nice prop sword for every occasion.

Xena Warrior Princess

Ever since I watched the original TV show as a child with my mom, Xena has been a huge role model and my personal hero. She was strong, smart and wasn't afraid of anything. I wonder why it took me thirteen years to finally cosplay as her. While the original costume was completely made of real leather, I used faux pleather for my version. I simply wrapped my mannequin in duct tape to get a pattern for the corset. I also studied several tutorials on how to sew a corset. All armor pieces like her iconic breastplate, shoulder pads and the bracers were made out of black Worbla. I used the same material for her chakram and the sword, though with a balsa wood core. I got my wig from a cosplay store online and gave it a nice cut and styling. Xena is a super fun costume to wear! I can jump around, scream, swing my sword and run around like a complete goofball while wearing this outfit. And the best part: My mom absolutely adores me as the Warrior Princess!

A Complete Costume From Start to Finish

After all these armor and prop examples I think it's time to finally show you how I made one of my favorite costumes from start to finish. It's always good to see what goes into making an entire cosplay and understand the whole picture. The best motivation to bring a character to life is to choose something that you're a huge fan of. I'm a gamer and love all kinds of video games, so cosplaying someone from *League of Legends* was only a matter of time. The game itself is set in a colorful fantasy world and has many quirky characters with stunning armor designs. I love purple and teal, strong female characters and gigantic weapons, so I chose Dark Valkyrie Diana.

It's usually easy to find good reference material for heroes from video games. After a quick Google search I was able to get various screenshots and concept art of her costume from many different angles, and I even discovered a website where I could rotate her 3-D model around. Good references will give you many ideas of how to create specific costume pieces and even allow you to discover the tiniest details.

I often start with the most fun part of a project: making all the cool armor pieces. In Diana's case I also experimented a little bit with her design. Cosplay is not always about copying a fictional character and setting him into reality. It's also a lot about your own creativity and how you choose to interpret and translate a design.

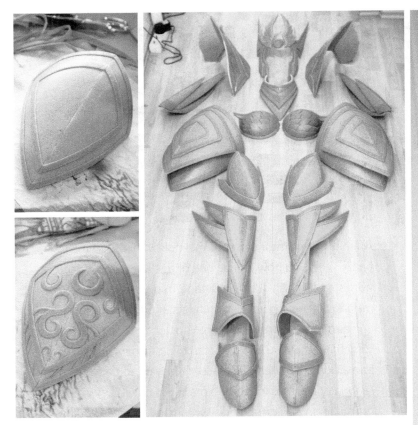

Assembling the Armor Pieces

At the end of the day you're creating the costume for yourself, so you are allowed to do that however you want. I played around with different kinds of ornaments and swirls since I wanted to add my own personal touch. My idea was to make the costume a little more interesting by adding more decorations. After some research I noticed that it didn't really work with her personality. Diana is a dark, cold and calculating assassin, somebody who couldn't care less about having pretty armor. So I made only a few additional lines and refined my idea of her by adding some battle damage instead.

As you can see, I chose to use Worbla for this project. It really depends on your personal preference, but in my case I feel more comfortable working with this thermoplastic instead of EVA foam. I'm pretty sure that there are other cosplayers who have made Diana completely out of foam though.

Once I figured out how I wanted to make her armor pieces, I started building the full set. Everything you see here is craft foam/Worbla sandwich pieces just like I showed you in my very first bracer example. My schedule allowed me only two weeks of time for this project, so I had to hurry. To speed up my crafting process I used two heat guns at once and built my costume pieces almost like an assembly line. If you're ever in a hurry, it helps to keep similar work steps stacked together. You'll get a nice routine, make fewer mistakes and be able to bring things together much faster.

Sewing the Fabric

The fabric part was a little bit trickier. I've had my fair share of problems with sewing machines, and I'm always a bit worried about working with textiles. Stretchy fabrics are luckily very forgiving and don't require perfect patterning or flawless sewing skills. I used a thin, teal-colored Lycra that is often used for swimwear. The trim was a golden metallic fabric, while a fine see-through mesh material completed my bodysuit. Both had to be just as stretchy as the Lycra of course. The pattern for the whole sewing part was made from an old swimsuit that I traced directly onto my costume fabric. Everything went pretty smoothly from there, and luckily there weren't many cloth parts that needed to be done for the costume afterwards.

Painting and Finishing the Armor

Once I finished all my costume pieces, I covered them in five layers of white glue, piece after piece. It always takes a little time until the glue layer is dried, but you can continue with the next piece while you wait for the first to dry and so on. I got all of my sixteen armor parts primed in no time. For the paint job I mainly used acrylics. However, this time I wanted to have a magical shimmering effect for my purple. I found a few cans of effect sprays at my local hardware store that fit perfectly. After covering all my armor parts with a dark mix of black and blue, I added gradients in a brighter blue. On top of that layer came a coat of my new transparent effect spray. This transformed my paint job into an amazing, almost holographic effect that switched from blue to purple depending on the viewing angle. Finally, I used a mix of gold and bronze to cover the edges and sealed my paint job with satin gloss varnish.

Designing the Details

Some important and unmistakable design elements of Diana are purple wings with pink tips on her back and her hip armor plates. I ordered around 2 lbs. (1kg) of white goose feathers over the Internet, cut them to the right shape and dyed them with the right fabric dye in an old cooking pot filled with hot water and some color. The longer I cooked the feathers on low heat, the more they turned blue or purple. I did not set an alarm and worked only by guessing, so every single feather was colored a little bit differently. This way the final wings turned out very natural. I have to be honest: It can be very dangerous to eat something from the kitchen of a cosplayer. You never know what has been in a frying pan, oven or plate. Just ask beforehand, or leave it be since sometimes it's better not knowing. Now all I had to do was hot glue every single feather to a piece of Worbla and attach them to the back of my costume with string.

Creating the Wig

Next up was Diana's wig. I had pretty long hair back when I made the costume, but dying it blue with purple tips was still out of the question for me. Instead I decided to buy a high-quality blue wig and sewed in purple wefts afterwards. I thinned the hair quite a lot at the bottom to give it a more naturally grown look. Bought wigs sometimes come in a rough cut, so you have to style and cut them. I also sewed four tiny buckles to the forehead area and placed their counterparts on Diana's headpiece. This was an easy and fast way to make the mask stay on my face while still allowing it to have a bit of free space and not rub against my face all the time.

Creating a Prop for Travel

Traveling with my costumes and actually being able to fit them into a tiny suitcase is essential for me. The final decision about my next project often is not about how much I like a character, but if I'm able to bring the costume onto a plane. This makes having huge props really difficult. Since Diana's blade is almost as tall as me, I had to find a solution.

After a little bit of experimenting and research, I decided to separate the blade into three parts. I cut the base out of 10mm EVA foam and hot glued a few PVC pipes of different diameters inside. Their counterparts were slightly smaller and I was able to slide them into each other, thus connecting all three parts. Afterwards I carved the foam, covered it with Worbla and added a few magnets for additional safety.

Sometimes it can be hard to get a really smooth and even surface. To get rid of all the bumps, I covered the blade in five layers of gesso, a thick acrylic primer. Today I would probably just use spray filler, but back then I didn't know it existed. Once my coats had dried, I hit the blade with my orbital sander and got a nice and shiny base for the paint job. I had no problem fitting this three-part blade into my suitcase.

I only had to connect all of my costume pieces and Diana was basically done!

Making a Final Photo

Dark Valkyrie Diana turned out to be one of my favorite costumes. Carrying her gigantic prop for a whole day and moving around packed full of armor was not easy, but it made me appreciate her strength even more. I simply love turning myself into this dark and mysterious lady. Luckily, I wasn't the only one who was really fond of her. Sabrina Schmitt, a friend of mine and a very talented photographer and digital artist, accepted the challenge and wanted to bring my Diana to life through a photo manipulation. She came over to my place and we took a few pictures in front of a big white background using two small lights. While the original photo looked really plain and boring, she did some magic on her computer.

First she replaced the bland background with stunning stock mountain formations, then she transformed my simple wig into a waving cascade of fluorescent blue and placed me in front of the glaring moon on a windy night. I think it's really close to the original reference artwork, and she did a truly amazing job! For me a couple of amazing pictures and friendships like these are the best reward a cosplayer can get for endless hours of work.

Photo by Sabrina Schmitt: facebook.com/SabrinaSchmittArt

What's Next?

So now that we've reached the end of the how-to section of this book, you're probably wondering what you should do with your finished costume. Go out there! Show it to people and have fun acting just like

the character. Bringing a cosplay to life doesn't just mean creating the outfit and then goofing around in it. In my opinion, a proper photoshoot at a nice location can really do your hard work much more justice. Re-creating your favorite scene with the right background, props, ambient light and a memorable pose can be a cool adventure on its own. Over time, the cosplay scene developed a whole culture about hobby photography. Friends usually do private photoshoots at conventions or during the weekends.

There are also countless professional and hobby cosplay photographers who are running around on convention floors and would love to get a photo of you. Some of your friends probably have a nice camera as well and would love to help you out. My friends usually give me their photos so I can edit them myself. Even professional photo editing software is easy to come by these days with programs like Adobe Lightroom® or Photoshop®. It's all about having fun being creative.

Try to collaborate with other artists, publish your costume progress online or even write full tutorials like I do. Cosplay is so much more than just creating a cool outfit. So go out there and do things with it. The possibilities are endless!

Photos by Christine Hemlep

Make or Buy Armor Underwear

You may find yourself wondering what you should wear under your armor. If you haven't touched a sewing machine before, then the easiest way is probably to buy something. Websites like eBay and Amazon will help you find all kinds of fitting pieces like bodysuits, jumpsuits, tights and even shapewear in all kinds of colors and sizes. There is nothing wrong with simply ordering a piece online. It's not easy to master armor making, prop making and sewing all at the same time. Did you know that you can even order custom-printed bodysuits with cool chain mail or space armor textures? The Internet is full of cool stuff; you just need to know where to find it.

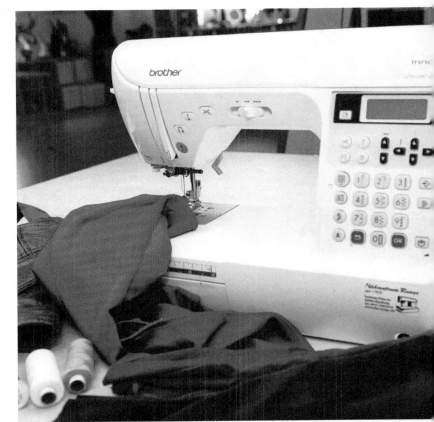

Grow Your Workshop

I showed you a few of my favorite tools and materials and explained how to create some really cool stuff. That's basically just the tip of the iceberg though. There is so much more to explore—woodworking and leather working, sculpting, casting and molding, electronics—just to name a few. Go try all of them, and with every project, you'll learn something new and improve your skills. I am sure there will be nothing stopping you. So go out there, get more tools, buy more books and try out new ways to create things. Over time your workshop will grow and fill up with more tools that will make creating costumes a lot easier. Who knows where this will take you in life?

Discover New Techniques

You don't need to limit yourself to only following tutorials. Why not discover something yourself? By learning from other artists and exploring the Internet, you'll find countless new ideas for creativity. Every day there are new tools to try out—3-D home printers, CNC routers or laser cutters. Why not try out LEDs and electronics? They might be intimidating at first, but learning new things is just as exciting as holding a fancy new prop in your hand. There are so many possibilities, and if you're just starting to experiment, you may never want to stop again. Cosplay is an amazing hobby, and there are millions of passionate artists all over the world. The community is helpful, inspiring and a never-ending pool of ideas. Follow others' work and be inspired!

Participate in Contests

If you like the thrill of standing in front of a crowd or want to challenge yourself, then entering costume contests might be the thing for you. Pretty much every convention runs at least one of them, while others even have all kinds of different competitions spread over the weekend. Costume contests are often promoted with cash prizes, merchandise, crafting supplies or even fully paid trips to other countries. Despite all the cool loot you can get, you should participate mainly because of the fun aspect. These events are the best way to meet amazing artists backstage when you otherwise would not have had the chance to meet. You're able to share ideas and knowledge in a calm area and might even find a friend or two. You shouldn't expect to win—just have an amazing time with the other contestants and get an inspirational boost by seeing their work in person.

Photo by: CoolADN

Gladiators with Hyperion Set

from *Aion - Tower of Eternity*

Fabio Rupel and Sabrina Lettiero | Italy
facebook.com/HydraSylesiaCos

"Cosplay for us is a world that unites our greatest passions—video games, manga, anime and movies. With cosplay we discovered that, even for a short time, we could become the comic book and video game heroes that we always wanted to be since childhood. The look of people who recognize the character you play, all the wonderful people we met during the years, the days spent designing and creating costumes, wounds and tears, competitions, disappointments and victories . . . all this is cosplay!"

Photo by Elisabetta Sbisà

Costume Inspiration Gallery

I created all the pieces in this book to introduce you to some easy techniques and affordable materials. Hopefully you now have at least some ideas for how to turn a boring piece of foam into shiny armor. And just like me, there are many other artists creating costumes every single day.

Over the following pages I'll show you just a fraction of our amazing cosplay community. Sadly, there is only so much space in this book that we can dedicate to them. I also asked these amazing artists to write a short answer to the question: "What is cosplay for you?"

Please enjoy their work and let them inspire you with their endless creativity and passion. Exploring and following the creations of others is a huge inspiration for my own work as well and keeps me motivated every single day.

Please make sure to check out all the other submitted work at: kamuicosplay.com/epiccosplay.

General Zod

from *Man of Steel*

Eric Browning | United States
facebook.com/ericbrowningcosplay

"Cosplay for me has been a means to an end for uniting the left and right halves of my brain in an enjoyable hobby and for meeting like-minded new people. I put together my artistic and technical skills into detailed and accurate cosplay, which has led to all sorts of opportunities like judging and panels. I love to help friends out when they are stuck or just need a few ideas to get them moving on their own cosplay. I guess you could call me an artistic costumed problem solver."

Photo by Trevor Nielson

Inquisitor Evangelyne Karlzan

from *Warhammer 40k*

Melody Tripp | United States
facebook.com/melodywisecosplay

"Cosplay is my outlet for bringing ideas to life by becoming that idea. I love to draw inspiration from the inspired; teams of artists pour their passion into creating compelling characters and stories, and that emotional investment is felt by fans everywhere. Every costume is a puzzle without instructions, giving me the chance to learn materials or processes that I've never tried before. With everything I've learned along the way, cosplay allows me to help others realize their own inspiration by sharing my knowledge through local armor-building workshops."

Beyond the Darkroom Photography

Alpha Toothless Gijinka

from *How to Train Your Dragon 2*
Gladzy Kei I Canada
facebook.com/GladzyKei

"Cosplay is a beautiful art form that challenges individuals to become the best part of themselves through dressing up as their favorite character! It's a very creative outlet for nerds, geeks, otakus and all sorts of fandoms. Cosplaying serves as a gateway for me to become friends with incredible and talented people that share the same passion as I do. It's amazing how far some people have come through this bizarre and fantastic hobby. I feel so blessed and grateful to be able to inspire and to be inspired by these cosplayers. And also, cosplaying is so much FUN!"

Original photo by William Tan | Editing by Sabrina Schmitt

Brienne of Tarth

from *Game of Thrones*

Megan Heikkinen aka Galacticat |
United States
facebook.com/galacticatcosplay

"For me, cosplay is a life-changer. I've found
something I'm truly passionate about, something
that fulfills my desire to create, but that also
pushes my limits and challenges me as I'm
continually required to learn new skills. I've
met so many people and made tons of friends,
not just locally, but around the country and
even around the world. It's helped me with my
self-esteem and body confidence, while at the
same time it's motivated me to get healthier and
fit. My life would be quite different had I never
discovered this amazing hobby."

Photo by dwrd Studios

Night Elf Hunter

from *World of Warcraft*
Ashley O'Neill l Canada
facebook.com/OshleyCosplayDiary

"Cosplay gives me an artistic outlet to express my obsession with my favorite characters! I really enjoy the creative process behind figuring out how to approach a fictional costume and then crafting it to be worn in real life. Cosplay fuels my creativity and challenges me to try new techniques and hone my craftsmanship. The social aspect of cosplay is really important to me as well, and I have met the most amazing people through this hobby. Right now, having the opportunity to cosplay with my friends helps me stay motivated, inspired and dedicated to having fun!"

Studio Henshin Photography

King Loki

from *Marvel*

worn by Katelyn Jones Cosplay
Made by Eric Jones aka Coregeek | United States
coregeek.net

"This might sound trite—but friendship is what cosplay means for me. There is such great camaraderie in the community. I've met so many incredibly talented and helpful people (in person and online) through this hobby. My skill as a maker grows because so many people are willing to help by creating content that benefits me. In return I attempt to do the same. Plus, it's a blast to wear a costume you've put many hard hours into and bring that character to life. I love seeing the surprise on a person's face when they look at me as their favorite character. It's a special bond we share for that moment."

Photo by Eric Jones

Rena

from *Elsword*

Sweet Angel I Italy
sweetangelcosplay.com

"Cosplay is to portray a character
you like, and it is a challenge for
yourself. You can learn many
things and become proud of yourself. Cosplay is a wonderful hobby
that permits you to meet and make
new and long-lasting friendships
with people all over the world. It's
pure magic."

Photo by Dizzymonogatari

Lieutenant Allison Jakes

from *Privateer Press: Warmachine*

Allie Rose-Marie Leost | Canada
facebook.com/AllieCatCos

"Cosplay is loving your body for the beautiful human, elf, orc or mermaid you are. It's pushing your artistic abilities out of your comfort zone and pursuing goals that are unique, creative and keep you constantly challenged. It's rising above jealousy and bullying and being kind to those from all walks of life. It's not about using others as a means to an end but to the beginning of lasting friendships. Finally and foremost, it's making the things you love into the things you love to be and not giving a fluff what anybody thinks because you are a fabulous, wonderful, remarkable you."

Photo by Vancosplay Photography

Wrath Sonya

from *Heroes of the Storm*

Tiff Nguyen aka Honeyboba | United States
tiff.cc

"Cosplay is being able to escape from your normal, geeky-looking self by transforming into an alter ego. Cosplay is wanting something in-game so bad that you end up making it in real life. Cosplay is rushing to meet deadlines while throwing the occasional tantrum here and there (I'm kidding! I think . . .), but you overcome obstacles and learn from your mistakes along the way. Cosplay is a lot of things, but most importantly it's a good reminder to tell yourself that it's okay to be a really, really big kid where you can have fun and not care what people think."

Photo by FiveRings Photography

Magic Armor Link

from *The Legend of Zelda: Twilight Princess*
Carolyn Doerr aka Rinkujutsu | United States
facebook.com/Rinkujutsu- 141217807908 0819

"For me, cosplay is an art form that allows me to utilize various handcrafting techniques to make one unified creation. Cosplay is not necessarily about making costumes, but for me it is. I love how costume making involves dozens of skills, unlike other handcrafting hobbies that involve just a few. While I do like wearing costumes based on my favorite characters, my true enjoyment comes from the intensive handcrafting. I made my first costume on a whim almost five years ago, not knowing that cosplay existed until later. The crafting experience was so enjoyable that I decided to continue."

Photo by Nude Carbon Studios

Thank You!

At this point I want to thank you, dear reader! Thank you for following me through this book and joining me on this adventure. I hope I was able to give you at least a little glimpse at how wonderful, creative and captivating this hobby can be.

For me cosplay has been a never-ending source of inspiration, fun and passion for over a decade now. Your support is the reason why I can keep on dreaming. I truly hope you liked this little crafting guide, got some new ideas and have been inspired to tackle your own project soon. As always, don't be scared to try out new things and go forward. You never know what the future has in store for you!

ADVANCED COSPLAY
ARMOR MAKING
HELMETS & PAULDRONS

BY SVETLANA QUINDT

Helpful Resources

I've already mentioned some places where you can find all kinds of different tools and materials, though I want to use this page to leave you a few helpful links as well:

kamuicosplay.com

On my personal pages you'll find all my other crafting books as well as countless other helpful videos, tutorials and guides.

cosplaysupplies.com

This is the perfect place to get Worbla, foam, feathers, sculpting materials and all kinds of different crafting materials. It's the number one cosplay distributor in the United States and Canada.

cast4art.de/distribution

If you're having trouble finding a vendor for Worbla, check out the main distributor's website for help to find a store.

arda-wigs.com

Getting the right wig might take longer than you think. With a wide range of cuts, styles and colors, arda-wigs has the right wig for pretty much every occasion.

foammart.com

FoamMart is the perfect place to get all kinds of foams in different thicknesses, densities and colors. Additionally, they offer glues and primers, so make sure to check them out if you're from the states.

cosplayshop.be

The gray foam you saw in this book is actually from a shop in Belgium called cosplayshop.be. There are more awesome cosplay crafting shops in Europe, so make sure to check them out:

minque.nl

mycostumes.de

cosplaymat.com/fr

coscraft.co.uk

You can always find materials on Amazon, eBay and from your local craft and hardware stores, too.

Index

a content + ecommerce company

Other fine IMPACT Books are available from your favorite bookstore, art supply store or online supplier. Visit our website at fwcommunity.com.

20 19 18 17   5 4 3 2

DISTRIBUTED IN CANADA BY FRASER DIRECT
100 Armstrong Avenue
Georgetown, ON, Canada L7G 5S4
Tel: (905) 877-4411

DISTRIBUTED IN THE U.K. AND EUROPE
BY F&W MEDIA INTERNATIONAL LTD
Pynes Hill Court, Pynes Hill, Rydon Lane, Exeter, EX2 5AZ, UK
Tel: (+44) 1392-797680
Email: enquiries@fwmedia.com

ISBN 13: 978-1-4403-4516-6

Edited by **Beth Erikson**
Designed by **Geoff Raker and Clare Finney**
Production coordinated by **Jennifer Bass**
Front cover photograph by **Jay Tablante**
Back cover photograph by **Sabrina Schmitt**

Disclaimer

Photo by Darshelle Stevens: darshellestevens.com

About the Author

Svetlana Quindt was born in Angren, Uzbekistan, but moved with her family to Germany when she was five years old. She started making costumes in 2003 and hasn't stopped since. In 2013 she started doing cosplay as her full-time job. She has traveled around the world attending conventions. See more of her work at www.kamuicosplay.com.

Metric Conversion Chart

To convert	to	multiply by
Inches	Centimeters	2.54
Centimeters	Inches	0.4
Feet	Centimeters	30.5
Centimeters	Feet	0.03
Yards	Meters	0.9
Meters	Yards	1.1

Ideas. Instruction. Inspiration.

Download FREE weapon patterns at impact-books.com/costume-making-guide.

Check out these IMPACT titles at impact-books.com!

IMPACT-BOOKS.COM

- ✔ Connect with your favorite artists
- ✔ Get the latest in comic, fantasy and sci-fi art instruction, tips and techniques
- ✔ Be the first to get special deals on the products you need to improve your art